The Lords Leverhulme

Their lives, their families and their homes

Part I

The Life of Lady Lever

by Gavin Hunter

To my wife, Joy, without whose support
and encouragement
I would never have got this far.

Researched, written, designed and published by Gavin Hunter, Wirral 2013.
Copyright © Gavin Hunter 2013. Updated 2nd Edition 2018
Printed by Book Printing UK, Remus House, Woodston, Peterborough PE2 9BF

ISBN 978-0-9576933-0-2

Introduction

Beginning with the biography "Lord Leverhulme by his Son" published in 1927, a great deal has been written about William Hesketh Lever, the first Lord Leverhulme. Relatively little has been published about the second and third Viscounts who succeeded to the title.......... or about the rest of their families.

As honorary historian and archivist to the Leverhulme family it has been my ambition for some time now to address these omissions, put right any misinformation, and fill in some of the gaps about the first Viscount and his life.

Lasting many years, it has proved a daunting task which has threatened never to reach completion, while others have successfully completed and published their work. Therefore, spurred on and encouraged by the imminent anniversary of Lady Lever's death, I have decided to publish the work in three parts. This first part is devoted almost entirely to the life of Elizabeth Ellen Lever, Lady Lever, after whom the beautiful Art Gallery and Museum in Port Sunlight is named. Subsequent parts will unveil new aspects of the first Lord Leverhulme, his parents, his brother James Darcy Lever, and his eight sisters. The last part will introduce the hitherto neglected subject of the second and third Viscounts and their achievements.

I wish to express my appreciation for the generous support I have received from the members of the Leverhulme family, the trustees and staff of the Leverhulme Estate, and a whole variety of archives and individuals. I am particularly grateful to the staff at the Port Sunlight Village Trust, the Lady Lever Gallery, Unilever Archives, and the Bolton and Bury Archives. My special thanks go to fellow local historian Brian Mills in Bolton, and on Wirral to Stuart Irwin, Sarah Lynch, Ian Boumphrey, and to my editor and friend, Margaret Crawford.

My final thanks go to my late wife, Joy, without whose support I could never have got this far, and to whom I dedicate this work.

The vast majority of the historical pictures are from the Leverhulme family's private collection, many of which were taken by local photographer, George Davies, who was the son of William's coachman.

The portraits of William and Elizabeth Lever by Luke Fildes, the painting of Lady Lever by Maude Hall Neale, and the portrait busts of Elizabeth and William Lever are included by courtesy of National Museums Merseyside (Lady Lever Art Gallery, Port Sunlight).

The cover is based on a picture by local Wirral photographer, Phil Marsden.

Gavin Hunter
24th July 2013

Elizabeth Ellen Lever
by Mrs Maud Hall Neale

Contents

Elizabeth Ellen Lever, William
Hesketh Lever, and their son
William Hulme Lever, aged
18, in 1905 outside their home
at Thornton Manor.

Elizabeth Ellen
Lady Lever

'She cultivated only noble thoughts, loving words, and generous deeds'

……..These are the words on the side of the tomb of Elizabeth Ellen Lever, the wife of William Hesketh Lever, the co-founder of Lever Brothers and Port Sunlight. The inscription disappeared from view when William was laid to rest alongside his beloved wife some twelve years after she died. Reunited in death, they were companions for over fifty years, only separated when she passed away after a very short illness in 1913 in the fortieth year of their marriage.

She became 'Lady Lever' when William was made a baronet in 1911 – hence the name of the gallery dedicated to her memory. She never did enjoy the title of Lady Leverhulme which only came about when William was made a peer of the realm in 1917. He combined his name with her maiden name, Hulme, in her honour creating his new title, Baron Leverhulme of Bolton-le-Moors, later to become Viscount Leverhulme of the Western Isles – but that's another story.

William Lever is famous for the legacy he left behind: the factory and village at Port Sunlight, the great Leverhulme Estate on Wirral, the magnificent art collection in the Lady Lever Gallery, and the global business that grew into Unilever as we know it today.

Many of these were achieved during Elizabeth's lifetime, but one has to wonder if some of the later ventures such as his acquisition of the Outer Hebrides would have ever been undertaken had Elizabeth still been at his side.

Tradition suggests that behind every great man there is a great woman. Was that the case with Elizabeth and William? Perhaps not the power behind the throne, but Elizabeth Ellen was certainly the rock on whom William relied. At the time of her death the accolades to her were numerous. In a glowing tribute to her at the opening of The Lady Lever Gallery in 1922, nine years after she died, William described her as his 'greatest inspiration'.

"It has been truly said that a man who has had the luck to win the love of a true woman has won everything that life can give. Without this love in the home, life is only an apparition, a dream, and not a solid fact."

Affectionately referring to her as 'Lizzie', William had known Elizabeth since they first met as pupils at the little school in the cobbled street in Bolton where they both lived. She was nine months older than he was. Described by others as 'A gracious, kindly, gentle woman' and 'A tender frail little lady on the small side physically', she was certainly quite petite in stature. William was only five foot five inches tall himself, and, at four feet eleven, the top of Elizabeth's head barely came up to his shoulder.

Elizabeth clearly adored William, or 'Will' as she called him in her letters to him. She loved to be with him, missed him when he was away, worried about his health and his business, and was delighted to be there to greet him on his return from his many trips.

Elizabeth supported William in whatever he did, and took every opportunity to be with him, even when he had to get up very early in the morning to catch the seven o'clock train to Wigan in order to be there before the business opened at eight.

"Although he breakfasted at such an early hour, his wife always joined him at the table after having supervised the preparation of the breakfast. She had no greater joy in life than to see her husband starting the day's work cheerful and well nourished, and no day passed quickly for her when he was away. His home-coming at night was for her the great event of the day and the news he brought home of what the day brought forth was to her more interesting and thrilling than any other."

Elizabeth and William with their son, William Hulme, aged 5.

Elizabeth Ellen rejoiced in the love and success of her husband, and later in their son 'Willie', but there was also a lot of sadness in her life: as a young girl her two baby sisters and a baby brother died, she lost both her mother and father before she married William, and of the seven babies she gave birth to, only young William survived.

The Hulme Family Tree

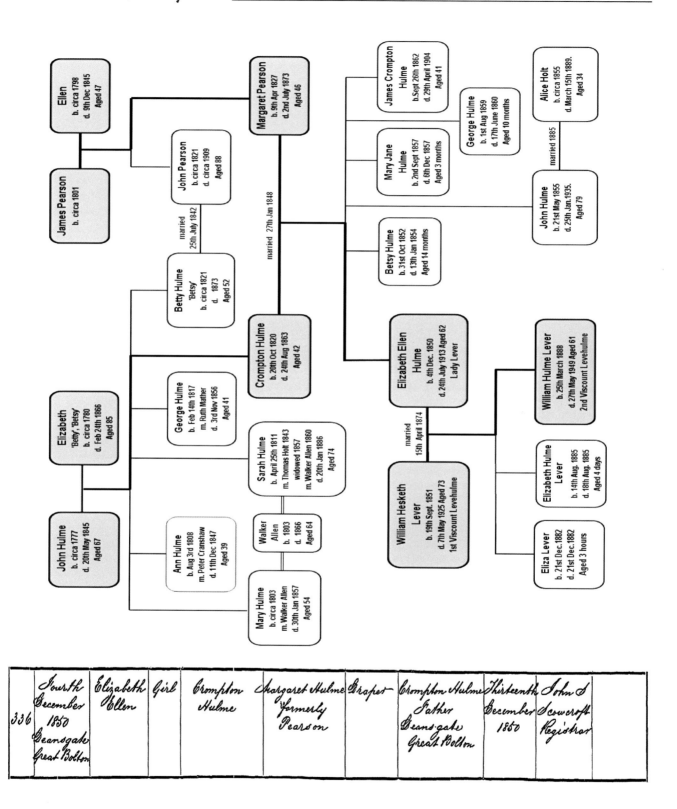

336	Fourth December 1850 Deansgate Great Bolton	Elizabeth Ellen	Girl	Crompton Hulme	Margaret Hulme formerly Pearson	Draper	Crompton Hulme Father Deansgate Great Bolton	Thirteenth December 1850	John S Scowcroft Registrar

Elizabeth Ellen was the daughter of Crompton and Margaret Hulme. Although she was later to live in the same street as her future husband William Lever, she was born at their home above Crompton's drapers shop in Deansgate in Bolton on December 4th 1850. She was apparently named after her two grandmothers: Elizabeth Hulme, known to the family as Betty, and her maternal grandmother, Ellen Pearson.

Her father, Crompton Hulme, was born in October 1820. He had grown up with his brothers and sisters on their father's farm at Stopes on the outskirts of Bolton. His father, John Hulme, was variously described over the years as a weaver, a farmer and a 'yeoman' - a term used to describe a small farmer owning and working his own land. John, Elizabeth's grandfather, died in 1845 aged 67, five years before Elizabeth was born and he was buried at Stand Chapel in Radcliffe. In 1861 at the age of 81 her grandmother, Betty, was still running the 6-acre farm with the help of one of her other granddaughters. She died aged 86 in February 1866, and was buried at Stand alongside her husband.

Crompton did not follow his father into farming; instead he became a 'retail and wholesale' linen draper. As a young man he served his apprenticeship as a draper with a Thomas Scholes at his premises in the centre of Bolton in Deansgate, where Crompton later set up his own drapery business just a few doors away. He would have started his apprenticeship when he was about fourteen, learning to cut and handle cloth and linen, and to deal with all the various linings, trimmings, buttons, threads, and other accessories required by tailors, dressmakers, and the general public. Apprenticeships usually lasted seven years and it would have been hard work. In return he probably received food, drink and lodging from Mr Scholes, and possibly a clothing allowance, but his training later enabled him to become a rich man in his own right. There were plenty of wealthy people around who wanted expensive fabrics for curtains, table and bed linen, and particularly clothing.

From the 1841 Census.......

In 1841 Crompton Hulme aged 20, together with two other apprentices, Edward Tudor (20) and John Bulcock (14), was working for Thomas Scholes, a draper with a business on Deansgate in Bolton.
Also living above the shop were Thomas's wife , Jane, and their two sons - John aged 6 and Robert aged 6 months - and a family servant, Sarah Pilkington.

The Hulme Family

Crompton had four sisters and a brother, so as a child Elizabeth would have been surrounded by lots of aunts, uncles and cousins. Crompton's eldest sister, Mary, married a cotton manufacturer, Walker Allen, from Radcliffe. They had seven surviving children and in later years Elizabeth kept in close contact with them all, in particular with their son, who was also called Walker. Mary died in 1857 and three years later Walker Allen senior married again. Keeping it in the family and complicating the family tree, he married another of Crompton's sisters. This time it was to Sarah Holt, who was already widowed herself.

Stand Chapel at Radcliffe near Bury, where Crompton Hulme was christened in January 1821, is the final resting place of many members of the Hulme family.

Another sister, Ann, married a Peter Cranshaw and three of their sons, Joseph, Moses, and Edward later served their apprenticeships under Crompton, going on to be drapers themselves. Brother George, a brickmaker, who acted as a witness at Crompton's wedding, married a Ruth Mather. George was also a witness at their sister Betty's wedding when she complicated the family tree even further by marrying Margaret's brother, John, in July 1842.

The Hulme family's birth and marriage records during this period are rather confused by the alternate uses of Elizabeth, Betty and Betsy for the same person, together with several transposition and recording errors, such as the fact that Hulme is sometimes recorded as Holme, and in 1851 Ellen is recorded as Helen. All this is further complicated by the various interfamily marriages, and by giving children the same names as their parents !

In the 1850s death was no stranger, certainly not to the Hulme family. Adult life expectancy in the area was generally down to a miserable average of twenty nine years, and infant mortality was very high. Buried in the small graveyard at Stand Chapel are twenty five children from the extended Hulme family, fourteen of whom lived less than a year.

Elizabeth's mother, Margaret Pearson, was born in Darcy Lever, Bolton in April 1827. Margaret's father, James, is variously described as a colliery manager, an agent and, at the time of her marriage to Crompton, as a 'steward'. Margaret had just one brother, John, a carpenter and boat builder. He married Crompton's sister, Betty and they had three children - James, George Taylor, and Elizabeth Ann. Like his cousins, James too later became Crompton's apprentice. Margaret's mother, Ellen, died in December 1845 two years before Margaret married Crompton.

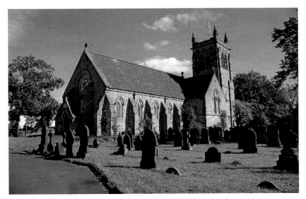

Margaret and Crompton were married on January 27th 1848 at St.Matthew's Church, Little Lever.
He was 27 and she was 20. Margaret's father, James Pearson, was one of the witnesses and the other witness was George Hulme, Crompton's brother.

The newly-wed Mr and Mrs Hulme went to live over his draper's shop in the centre of Bolton at No.1 Deansgate, where Elizabeth Ellen was born just over a year later. She was the eldest of their six children. Tragically three of them died as babies: Betsy who died of measles aged 14 months in 1854, Mary Jane from pneumonia aged 3 months in 1857, and George who died at just 10 months in 1860 of pyemia, a type of septicaemia. Their names are all recorded, together with their parents, on the Hulme family gravestone at Stand Chapel on the outskirts of Bury.

Thankfully, two of Elizabeth's brothers survived to adulthood: John Hulme, born in May 1855 at their Deansgate home, and James Crompton Hulme, born in September 1862 in nearby Wood Street.

Canon Slade.

The minister who performed the marriage ceremony, was a well-known Bolton philanthropist who dedicated his life to improving the conditions of the people of Bolton.

© Bolton Archives

Deansgate in 1832
Crompton's shop, where Elizabeth was born, occupied the far end of the four-storey building on the right. It was demolished in the early 1900s to make way for the Whewell building which now occupies the corner site.

From the 1851 Census.......

Deansgate today

The 1851 census records Crompton and Margaret living over the Deansgate shop with baby Elizabeth. Two of Crompton's nephews, Joseph and Moses Cranshaw, who were his apprentices, were living with them.

Crompton Hulme 1820 - 1863

This portrait of Crompton Hulme, Elizabeth's father, was commissioned by William and painted by Wolfram Onslow Ford in October 1902. It is apparently based on the picture on the left where he is seated with two colleagues, possibly his brothers. This is the only known photograph of Crompton who died more than ten years before Elizabeth married William.

This portrait of Margaret Hulme, Elizabeth's mother, was also painted by Wolfram Onslow Ford in 1902, some thirty years after Margaret died. Like that of her husband it also appears to be based on this, the only known photograph of Margaret.

The Lever Family Tree

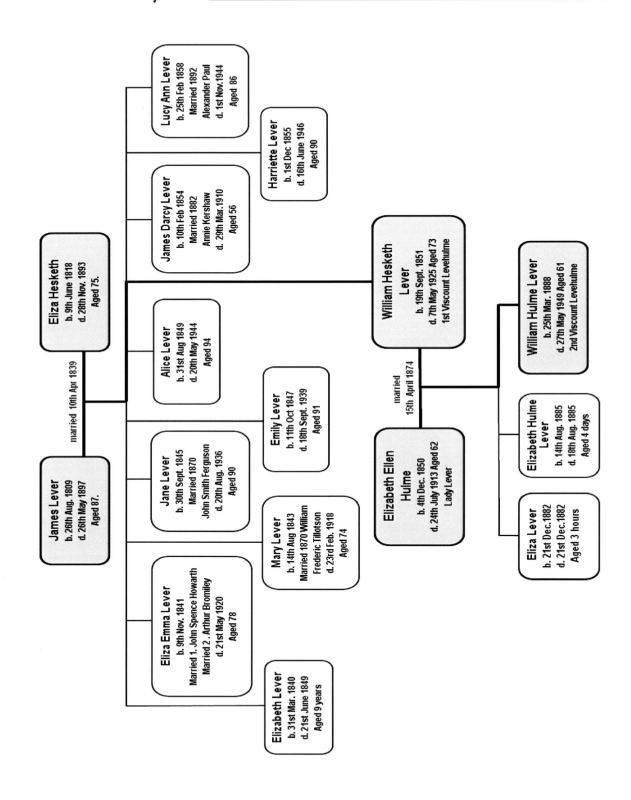

James Lever
b. 26th Aug. 1809
d. 26th May 1897
Aged 87.

married 10th Apr 1839

Eliza Hesketh
b. 9th June 1818
d. 28th Nov. 1893
Aged 75.

Elizabeth Lever
b. 31st Mar. 1840
d. 21st June 1849
Aged 9 years

Eliza Emma Lever
b. 9th Nov. 1841
Married 1. John Spence Howarth
Married 2. Arthur Bromiley
d. 21st May 1920
Aged 78

Mary Lever
b. 14th Aug 1843
Married 1870 William
Frederic Tillotson
d. 23rd Feb. 1918
Aged 74

Jane Lever
b. 30th Sept. 1845
Married 1870
John Smith Ferguson
d. 20th Aug. 1936
Aged 90

Emily Lever
b. 11th Oct 1847
d. 18th Sept. 1939
Aged 91

Alice Lever
b. 31st Aug 1849
d. 20th May 1944
Aged 94

James Darcy Lever
b. 10th Feb 1854
Married 1882
Annie Kershaw
d. 29th Mar.1910
Aged 56

Harriette Lever
b. 1st Dec 1855
d. 16th June 1946
Aged 90

Lucy Ann Lever
b. 25th Feb 1858
Married 1892
Alexander Paul
d. 1st Nov.1944
Aged 86

William Hesketh Lever
b. 19th Sept. 1851
d. 7th May 1925 Aged 73
1st Viscount Levehulme

married
15th April 1874

Elizabeth Ellen Hulme
b. 4th Dec. 1850
d. 24th July 1913 Aged 62
Lady Lever

Eliza Lever
b. 21st Dec.1882
d. 21st Dec.1882
Aged 3 hours

Elizabeth Hulme Lever
b. 14th Aug. 1885
d. 18th Aug. 1885
Aged 4 days

William Hulme Lever
b. 25th Mar. 1888
d. 27th May 1949 Aged 61
2nd Viscount Levehulme

Margaret and Crompton Hulme lived above the draper's shop for some twelve years before they moved out, by which time the business had expanded to occupy the former chemist's shop next door. While still retaining the Deansgate premises, in early 1860 they moved just two hundred metres door-to-door to their new home at No.15 Wood Street.

The terraced properties of Wood Street are deceptively large. In 1861, No.15 not only provided accommodation for Mr and Mrs Hulme, ten-year old Elizabeth and five-year old John, but also ten staff from the shop, and two servants.

Right opposite across the narrow cobbled street at No.16 lived the Lever family: James Lever, his wife Eliza, their eight daughters, Elizabeth, Eliza, Mary, Jane, Emily, Alice, Hariette, and Lucy, and their two sons William and James.....as well as a cook and a housemaid.

Mr and Mrs Lever had lived in Wood Street since 1842 when James, who originally served his apprenticeship in Bolton, moved back from Manchester to open up a retail grocery business. Their eldest daughter, Elizabeth, died the year before Elizabeth Ellen was born. The rest of the children survived to adulthood. The Lever family lived there for 22 years before they moved away in June 1864 to live in the premises above James' new wholesale grocery warehouse elsewhere in the town.

Wood Street, Bolton.
On the left is No.15 where Elizabeth lived with her parents and two brothers. On the right No.16 where William lived with his brother and eight sisters.

No. 16 Wood Street

This three-storey terraced property was home of Eliza and James Lever and their ten children from 1842 to 1864.

Looking out today across the narrow street from the front window of the Hulme's former home, we can see how the children of the two families became so closely acquainted.

James Lever
Retail and Wholesale Grocer

His former Wood Street home now displays a blue plaque identifying it as the birthplace of William Hesketh Lever.

The Aspinwall's School

Living at No.17, next door to the Hulme's new Wood Street home, were Joseph Aspinwall, a dental surgeon, and his three elderly spinster sisters, Elizabeth, Margaret and Ellen. The ladies were all teachers and ran a 'Ladies Seminary' in their home. William's biography clearly records the fact that he and Elizabeth went to the Misses Aspinwall's School together. As one of just five male scholars, he was a pupil there from when he was six until he was nine and would have left the school in the Summer of 1860, very soon after the Hulme family arrived in Wood Street.

Elizabeth was probably already attending the school before her family moved. Living just round the corner in Deansgate, and with his increasing wealth and status, her father Crompton would have been able to send Elizabeth to this 'Ladies Seminary' in Wood Street where she met her future husband.

The double fronted terraced home of the Hulme family at No.15 Wood Street, and beyond it No.17 where the Misses Aspinwall ran their Ladies Seminary.

Elizabeth with one of her friends. This is possibly William's sister, Alice, with whom Elizabeth developed a special friendship.

8-year old William in 1859.

Elizabeth's father, Crompton Hulme, died at their Wood Street home in August 1863 aged just 42 of 'fever of the brain' - possibly meningitis caused by bacteria which is often fatal. His death was registered by his sister, Betsy, who was there when he died.

At the time of his death Elizabeth was only twelve years old, John was eight, and little James was just eleven months old. Their father was buried at Stand Chapel alongside his infant children.

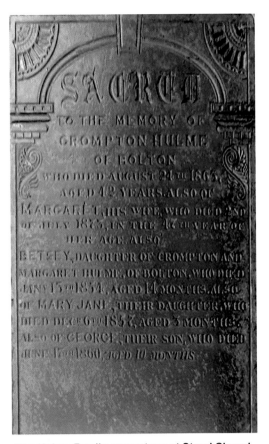

The Hulme Family gravestone at Stand Chapel.
On it are recorded the names of Crompton Hulme, his wife Margaret, and Elizabeth's two sisters, Betsy (14 months), Mary Jane (3 months), and her brother, George (10 months).
The gravestone marks the site of the new grave, repositioned when the chapel was extended in 1886.

Inheritance arrangements were very different at this time – in general sons inherited, daughters and wives did not. When he died, Crompton was a relatively wealthy man. His estate included his shop in Deansgate, the house in Wood Street, and several cottages in Bolton. He also owned a share of the 'Grundy Fold Estate', the family farm at Stopes in Little Lever which had been in the family for over 250 years, inherited from his father although his mother still continued to run it.

Few traces of the Grundy Fold Farm buildings survive from the time the Hulme family farmed the area.

Crompton died before both his mother and his wife but, under his will, his share in the farm was still to go to his eldest son John. Although his wife Margaret was still alive, control of his affairs passed to his executors: John Collyer, a 45-year old linen and woollen draper from Chorley, and John Pickup, a 40-year old woollen cloth manufacturer from Manchester. Neither appears to have been a friend or colleague from his apprenticeship days, so presumably they were both associates whom he had met through his business.

Margaret was to *'enjoy the use of his household goods, furniture, plate, linen and china, and to receive the income from his estate for the rest of her natural life'* – unless she remarried in which case she would receive £50 a year. Any residue of his estate was to be divided between the children after the youngest achieved the age of twenty one. This was later to lead to a dispute after Elizabeth's marriage to William, when the executors said that her father actually *'did not intend married daughters to take their income.'*

Moving to Southport

Widowed but financially secure, Margaret moved away from Bolton with the three children.

Initially they went to Radcliffe where Crompton's cousin, Walker Allen, lived but by 1866 they had moved to Southport. They lived first in a house on Princes Street, and then they moved to nearby Talbot Street where Margaret rented a large detached red-brick Victorian house called 'Nile Bank' which is still there today, though somewhat changed and re-numbered.

'Nile Bank'
The Hulme family's home in Southport.

William in 1897

In 1867, soon after Elizabeth had moved to Southport with her mother and two brothers, William became an apprentice in his father's grocery business. They still kept in touch, but their friendship was a secret from all but their very closest friends. Alice, William's sister who was one of Elizabeth's best friends, often carried messages between the two of them.

Travelling by train, William soon took every opportunity to go with Alice to Southport. He even made secret arrangements to meet Elizabeth in Chorley when she went to stay with her guardian, John Pickup, without whose consent Elizabeth had promised not to become engaged.

From Summer 1872 William, now approaching 21, wrote virtually every other day to his dearest Lizzie, and they were secretly betrothed in the September. Elizabeth's mother apparently teased her about her relationship with William, but never directly asked if they were engaged.

William's parents also tried to find out what was going on. So, to keep their relationship private from the people in Bolton, Elizabeth's letters to William were delivered care/of the Bolton Post Office.

Elizabeth and William formally announced their engagement on Saturday December 7th 1872. His father lent him the money for an engagement ring, which he later paid back by instalments.

Elizabeth Ellen Hulme

William Hesketh Lever

Elizabeth kept these two pictures in a gold locket.
They possibly date from the perod that she lived with her mother in Southport.

In late June 1873, nearly ten years after her husband had passed away, Margaret Hulme, together with Elizabeth and the two boys, moved back to Bolton. They went to live at No.5 Holly Bank, off Seymour Road, in Sharples on the outskirts of the town. This large house stands on Dormer Road in what is now Astley Bridge. Meanwhile, the previous month, William had moved with his parents to their picturesque new home at Harwood Lodge, some two miles outside Bolton.

When they moved back to Bolton, Margaret must have already been very ill for she died less than a fortnight later on July 2nd, aged just 46. Her death certificate reveals that she had been suffering from 'phthises', a name used at the time to describe any wasting disease. Sometimes described as consumption, it most likely meant that she was suffering from tuberculosis, which may have been why she had moved to Southport in the first place. She was buried three days later at Stand Chapel alongside her husband and infant children.

Under the watchful eye of the housekeeper, and their guardian John Pickup, Elizabeth and her brothers continued to live at Holly Bank.

Their mother had passed away just six months after Elizabeth and William had announced their engagement, and ten months before they were to be married. Elizabeth was now twenty two and was the eldest of the children. John was eighteen, and James was twelve. Margery Holland, their housekeeper from Southport, had moved to Bolton with them and remained as their housekeeper for many years. At first she was housekeeper to all three of them, then to John and James, and finally just to James. In total Margery looked after James for nearly forty years, from when he was just a small child in Southport.

On February 12th 1874 William leased No.2 Park Street, Bolton for £51 a year. This double fronted end-terrace property was just along the street from where his sister Mary and her husband had made their first home some four years earlier. William immediately set about preparing the house for Elizabeth's and his occupation two months later.

Elizabeth and William's marriage

On April 15th 1874 Elizabeth Ellen Hulme aged 23 of Holly Bank, Sharples, Little Bolton married William Hesketh Lever aged 22 of Park Street, Bolton at St George's Road Congregational Church, Little Bolton. This was the same church where William's father was a deacon and superintendent of the Sunday Schools.

The week before they were married William had bought the wedding ring for £1.2s.0d *(£1.10p)*, together with a gold pearl bracelet for £11.15s.0d *(£11.75p)*, and a silver bouquet holder for 15s 6d *(77½p)*, from Gilbert & Pinders, Silversmiths and Jewellers of Bolton.

On the day of the wedding he hired a whole fleet of cabs and carriages from Edmund Holden's, the local 'Omnibus and Coach Company', to ferry the guests backwards and forwards between the church, the railway station, Elizabeth's house in Sharples, and his parents' home at Harwood.

Elizabeth herself travelled to the wedding in a carriage pulled by a pair of grey horses. It must have been quite a spectacular affair. Sadly there are no wedding pictures.

St George's Road Congregational Church, Bolton, where Elizabeth and William were married on April 15th 1874.
Still there today but now without its steeple which was removed some years ago.

No.5 Holly Bank in Sharples where Elizabeth lived with her brothers after the family returned from Southport.

Elizabeth travelled to the wedding in a carriage, known as a 'brougham' pulled by a pair of grey horses.

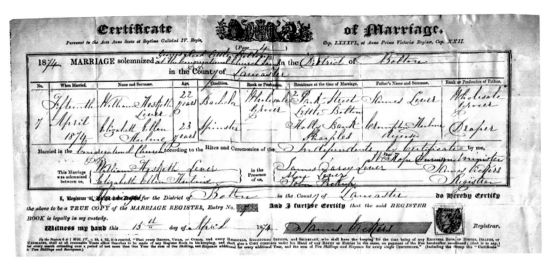

The wedding ceremony was conducted by two ministers: the Rev. W. Hope Davison of Bolton, who had baptised both William and Elizabeth, and the Rev. John Chator, the minister of West End Chapel, where the Hulme family had worshipped whilst they lived in Southport. The witnesses were William's brother, James Darcy Lever, their sister Alice, and John Pickup, Elizabeth's guardian who probably 'gave her away'. The bridesmaids included John Pickup's 16-year old daughter Emily.

The flowers for the wedding were supplied by Victoria Nursery, Cope Bank, Halliwell, near Bolton at a cost of £2.15.6d (£2.77½ p). That was more than twice as much as William had paid for the wedding ring the week before.

The Rev. Hope Davison who conducted the marriage ceremony.

After the wedding there was a 'wedding breakfast', which was supplied by a Mrs Hamer, and then the guests were taken in two small horse-drawn omnibuses, paid for by Elizabeth's cousin Walker Allen, for a picnic at Worsley near Manchester.

William's mother later wrote that she was *"very much disappointed with Mrs Hamer's provision for breakfast. It was not equal to either Mary's or Jane's and if the charge is what she said, it will be a great imposition. We had quite as nice a spread at Worseley, omitting the bride cake jelly and trifle, and what had vexed me most of all Mrs Hamer did not give Margaret or Mrs Woodhead any dinner or rather breakfast although the waitresses had theirs but took any scraps away. I hope whoever pays will tell her about it.*
We saw several friends yesterday and they all thought Lizzie looked very nice indeed in white. I quite agree with them and no doubt you do the same."

In Mrs Lever senior's opinion, Mrs Hamer, the caterer, had obviously not done a very good job. Mary and Jane were William's older sisters who had been married three or four years earlier, and Margaret and Mrs. Woodhead were probably Eliza's own servants who were helping out at the wedding breakfast.

The Honeymoon

After their wedding, Elizabeth and William left later that day by train to spend a fortnight's honeymoon touring Devon and Cornwall.

They certainly showed a liking for grand hotels. Their first night en-route was spent at the North Western Hotel opposite Stafford Railway Station. Built in 1866, to provide accommodation for rail travellers, it offered all the latest facilities including a coffee room reserved for ladies, a billiard room, and kitchens on the second floor so guests would not be troubled by cooking smells.

The following day they visited Stratford upon Avon, *'the birthplace of the immortal bard'*, where they spent the night at The Shakespeare Family and Commercial Hotel.

Three nights at the Clifton Down Hotel, and three nights at the Posting House in Ilfracombe, were followed by two nights at The Royal Hotel in Plymouth, and four nights at 'Miss Mary Dingley's Private & Family Hotel', at *Beachfield House* on The Esplanade at Penzance.

By the 29th, they were back in Devon at The Torbay Hotel, Torquay, and the last night of their honeymoon on the way home was spent at the Unicorn Hotel, Worcester, before they returned to Bolton.

Stafford's North Western Hotel.

Clifton Down Hotel.

The Royal Hotel, Plymouth.

The Torbay Hotel, Torquay.

No.2 Park Street, Bolton, leased for £51 a year, was Elizabeth and William's first home.

In his book 'Coming Clean', Andrew Knox recalls a conversation with Elizabeth who, when asked about her home in London said *"It's very nice, but it is like having two houses but no home."* In fact she and William lived in eleven different houses during their marriage.

Back from their honeymoon they went to live in their first home - a double-fronted end-terrace house in Park Street, Bolton. Like many of their early homes they rented it. William had already been living there for two months, getting it ready for their married life. Elizabeth is later reported to have said that she never lived in a house that did not echo to the sound of workmen……. and Park Street was no exception. William had new doors and fireplaces fitted, and spent over three hundred pounds on furniture, carpets and curtains, before they moved in.

The Park Street house was lit by gas and heated by coal fires. Downstairs there was a drawing room and dining room, and upstairs two bedrooms and a box room over the hall. At the back there was a yard with a small greenhouse, and in 1877 they were given planning permission for a conservatory.

They lived at Park Street for about six years, and during that time Elizabeth gave birth to three babies – a girl and two boys. Sadly none of them survived or was even given a name.

On February 3rd 1875 their first daughter was still-born just ten months after they were married. William bought a child's oak coffin from William Dorning, a cabinet maker of Bank Street, Bolton. The following day he took a cab to Stand Chapel where their infant daughter was laid to rest in the Hulme family grave.

Each year, on that day, Elizabeth would record her thoughts about their first child. In February 1895 she wrote *'I believe had she lived, today would have been our eldest daughter's 20th birthday. I wish it might have been, but He knows best'.*

Many years later, Rowland Evans, Lever's unofficial biographer wrote that Elizabeth's *"great grief was the death of her daughter when a baby"*. Surprisingly, although she regularly acknowledged the loss of their first baby, she never referred to any of the others. Perhaps the loss of that first child was more poignant than the rest.

Eighteen months later, in the early hours of the morning of October 1st 1876 Elizabeth, now 25, gave birth at Park Street to another still-born child, described by William as *'a fine boy'*. The following day William bought a lined oak coffin and, this time accompanied by his brother-in-law, W.F. Tillotson, once more took a cab to Stand Chapel where he *"buried our little one beside his sister"*.

The whole sad process was repeated yet again in 1877 when on August 24th another un-named child, recorded simply as the *'infant son of Mr Lever of Bolton'* was laid to rest in the Hulme family grave at Stand Chapel.

A new home in Bolton

In 1879 Elizabeth and William had a new house built. It was designed by their childhood friend, Jonathan Simpson, who was now a qualified architect. This was the first complete building that William had commissioned.

Called 'Lower House', this large detached house stood in three acres of grounds about two miles from their home in Park Street. They are recorded as living there in the 1881 census together with two servants, but it was not destined to be their home for very long.

'Lower House'

Lower House is still there on the corner of Chorley New Road and Lostock Junction Lane. It is now divided into multiple occupancy and several new houses occupy the original gardens.

William in 1877

As a partner in the family wholesale grocery business, William had extended their customer base beyond Bolton into the Wigan area. It was obvious to him that taking goods from Liverpool to Bolton and then back out to Wigan was both a waste of time and money. So he looked for premises in Wigan, and in 1877 bought the failing wholesale grocery business of Ormerod & Co and established the Wigan Branch of Lever & Co.

Lever's Wigan shop and warehouse

When the health of the manager of the Wigan branch began to deteriorate, William took over running the business there himself. Commuting everyday from Bolton by train meant getting up at 6.00am to be there in time to open up the shop at 8.00.
So just two years after moving into Lower House they sold it, and he and Elizabeth moved to a rented house in Wigan.

In 1881 Elizabeth and William moved from Bolton to Upper Dicconson Street in Wigan to be close to the business. With a rent of £40 a year, number twenty one was an end-of-terrace town house in an area occupied by local businessmen. A draper, grocer, tea dealer, cotton broker and their families were their new neighbours. Still there today, the two-storey house is deceptively large with attics and cellars throughout. Once again it would have resounded to the sound of workmen as William set about organising the alterations. Moulded cornices, dados, panelling, and fireplaces were added. Even an early form of air conditioning was installed.

Upper Dicconson Street, Wigan, where Elizabeth and William went to live in 1881

It was whilst they were living at Upper Dicconson Street that, on December 21st 1882, Elizabeth gave birth to their second daughter. Named Eliza, apparently after her grandmother, she was the first of two girls who were given names. Born two months premature, the baby only lived for three hours. William was with his wife at the birth, together with their Wigan physician, Dr.W.C.Barnish. [whose own son, Croudson William Barnish, was later to become managing director of Lever Brothers.]

Dr. William Croudson Barnish
Elizabeth's Wigan doctor

Two days later, William made that same sad trip to Stand Chapel. The Hulme family graves at Stand were now the final resting place of two of Elizabeth's grandparents, both her parents, her infant brother and two sisters, and four of her own children.

Four years later, in October 1886 Elizabeth attended the dedication of the re-built Stand Independent Church. Its extension had required the relocation of the Hulme family grave and not one of Elizabeth's children is recorded on the re-sited gravestone. Sadly the only record of their passing now lies in the church burial records.

The Stand Chapel register for the original Hulme grave. Started after the death of their second child, it records the burial dates of Crompton and Margaret Hulme, two of their children, three infant children of William Lever, all from Bolton, and finally Elizabeth and William's daughter, Eliza, who died in Wigan in December 1882 , but is incorrectly recorded as December 1883.

Returning to Bolton

William had sole charge of the Wigan branch of the Lever Wholesale Grocery which he ran for ten years before moving back to Bolton.

While they were still living in Wigan, he had rented another house on the outskirts of Bolton, quite near to their former home at Lower House. Their new home 'Westcombe' was a large detached property on Victoria Road built in 1881.

'Westcombe'

Although in later years, holidays were few and far between, in those early years of their marriage, William and Elizabeth did take regular holidays. In the summer of 1884 they cruised from Liverpool around the north coast of Britain calling at Oban, Stornoway in the Outer Hebrides, Stromness in Orkney, Aberdeen, and Newcastle.

This was the first time William saw the Outer Hebrides and years later in recalling that brief visit, he said *"I was greatly delighted by its natural beauty and variety of scenery, by its wonderful healthiness of climate and the charm and attraction of its people."* Already a wealthy man William even considered retiring from business and settling in the islands. One has to wonder whether, had Elizabeth still been alive thirty four years later, William would ever have embarked on his later attempt to industrialise the inhabitants of these remote Scottish islands, an encounter which will be explored further in a future publication.

It was following that trip, and while they were still living at Westcombe, that William, having rejected the idea of retiring, decided to become a soapmaker. The family business had been selling soap for some years but it was made for them by various third-party companies.

As sales increased, the manufacturers wanted to raise prices, so William decided to make the soap himself. In August 1885, together with his brother James, who had agreed to go into the venture with him, they founded the business of Lever Brothers. With £4,000 their father had loaned them, they took over the Warrington soapworks of Messrs Winsers & Company and began manufacturing Sunlight Soap, the brand developed and named by William himself.

The birth of a new company, but tragically the death of yet another child. On August 14th 1885 Elizabeth, now nearly 35, gave birth to their third daughter, Elizabeth Hulme Lever, at Westcombe. She died just four days later of 'prematurity convulsions'. Once again William was in attendance, and the death was certified by the same doctor, Dr Barnish from Wigan. This time baby Elizabeth was laid to rest in a new grave at Heaton Cemetery in Bolton, not far from their home. Although there had been other babies, the later census of 1911 only records two who died – the two who were given names: Elizabeth and her older sister Eliza.

Elizabeth Hulme Lever's grave in Heaton Cemetery, Bolton.

**'Lever House'
in Palmyra Square, Warrington.**

Presumably to get a break from the pressures of the new business, in August 1887 William and Elizabeth set off from Bristol on a tour of the West Country. Travelling in a very large and specially constructed caravan, capable of sleeping five and pulled by four horses, they toured the highways and byways of Devon and Dorset for several weeks.

They were joined on their journey first by Robert Kenyon and his wife, and later by Jonathan Simpson, both of whom were close friends from their time together at the Misses Aspinwall's school in Wood Street. While the men walked together through the countryside accompanied by 'Barrie' their magnificent St Bernard dog, Elizabeth went ahead with Sinah in the caravan to the next village to await their arrival. The cooking was done on an oil stove in the caravan, and several times local people mistook them for gypsies or circus show people !!

The following year, to be near their new factory during the week, William rented a Victorian terraced house in leafy Palmyra Square in the centre of Warrington. The house, now called Lever House, still bears a plaque erected in 1927 recording their stay there. For the next two years William and Elizabeth regularly shuttled back and forth between Warrington and Bolton.

As they returned to Bolton at the weekends, the house at Warrington seems to have been simply somewhere to sleep during the week. It was the only one that William never altered. The only rooms that were furnished were the kitchen, dining room and two bedrooms, while the drawing room was just used to store boxes and suitcases.

While they were in Warrington they were looked after by their devoted Welsh maid, Sinah, who used to travel backwards and forwards with them. She even went with them on a rather unusual holiday.

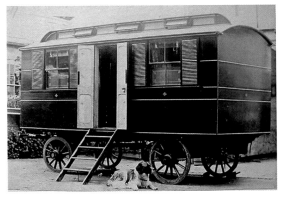

The caravan with Barrie, their St Bernard.

In later years holidays turned into business trips, and from early in their marriage Elizabeth was regularly involved in a variety of excursions and ceremonies – laying many foundation stones, opening churches and bazaars, handing out Sunday School prizes, planting trees, even on one occasion launching a ship. But in 1888, while they were still living at Westcombe, Elizabeth took part in what was probably one of the most significant events in William's business career.

The birth of Port Sunlight

Within two years of beginning to produce Sunlight Soap at Warrington, Lever Brothers had outgrown the factory, and they decided to build an entirely new factory. On March 3rd 1888, using a silver spade, Elizabeth ceremonially cut the first sod of the new works at Port Sunlight.

Handing the spade to Elizabeth, William Owen, the Warrington architect of the new factory said:

"I have been asked by Messrs. Lever Brothers to present, this very handsome spade to Mrs. W. H. Lever for the purpose of cutting the first sod. I don't know that there is any feature in life more pleasant than to see a wife taking an active and earnest interest in whatever her husband is doing. It has been my happy lot to have an intimate friendship with Mr. and Mrs. W. H. Lever, and I can assure you it has been the greatest possible pleasure to me to see the constant, earnest, and active interest which Mrs. Lever has shown in every step we have taken. You know you cannot arrive at buying land and setting up buildings without a great deal of work before we reach that point, and, during months of constant intercourse with Mr. Lever and his wife, every step we have taken has been watched with the greatest care and interest by Mrs. Lever."

The invitation, issued from the Warrington factory, to attend the ceremony of the cutting the first sod.

With the ceremony complete, Elizabeth said:
"The work I have done today has given me the greatest pleasure. In cutting this first sod, I wish you all success – success to the new works, success to the firm, and success to all interested in the sale and manufacture of Sunlight Soap."

The solid silver spade used by Elizabeth to cut the first sod of the Port Sunlight factory on March 3rd 1888.

Some of the party who attended the ceremonial start to the Port Sunlight factory, assembled near to the New Ferry landing stage.

Now thirty eight years old, Elizabeth was heavily pregnant when she performed the ceremony to mark the start of work on the Port Sunlight factory. In view of her previous history, there must have been considerable concern about her taking on this task, particularly as it involved a journey from Bolton to Liverpool, a trip by ferry and steam barge from Liverpool to the new factory site at Port Sunlight, and then back again across the Mersey for a celebration banquet – although from the transcriptions of the speeches after the banquet, it is possible that Elizabeth may not have stayed for the dinner.

The invitation to dinner at The Bear's Paw in Liverpool.

Presumably to keep an eye on his patient, Elizabeth's doctor, Dr Barnish, and his wife were there at the ceremony. He was apparently a doctor of some experience, and is reported to have devised a special regime involving the use of a water bed during her confinement to minimise the risk of her losing yet another baby.

But, despite all the risks, just three weeks later Elizabeth successfully gave birth to their son William Hulme Lever, who later described himself in his own book as 'their only surviving child'.

Elizabeth with baby William Hulme.

William junior was born on Palm Sunday, March 25th, 1888, at their 'Westcombe' home in Bolton. At long last, in their fourteenth year of marriage, William and Elizabeth had the joy of a child that was to survive into adulthood. Not surprisingly after all her problems, Elizabeth rejoiced in his birth, his childhood, and then his subsequent development to manhood, and she lavished every attention on him throughout the rest of her life.

William Hulme Lever was baptised on April 30th 1888 at Westcombe by the Rev. Hope Davidson, the former minister of the St George's Road Congregational Church who had married and baptised both Elizabeth and William. Like his father before him, their son was given his mother's maiden name as a second name in what had become a family tradition,

Moving from Bolton to Wirral

When Elizabeth got married, her brother John was 19 and James was still only 11. They continued to live with the housekeeper, Margery Holland, at Holly Bank in Bolton. They were still there in 1881 by which time John was described as an 'unemployed draper', having presumably decided not to carry on with the family business, and James was an 'architect's clerk'.

In April 1885 John, still living at Holly Bank and now described as 'gentleman', married Alice Holt of Park Hill Place, Chorley Old Road, Bolton.
Like William and Elizabeth, they too were married at St George's Road Congregational Church. At the time of their marriage Alice's father, James, was described as a 'yarn agent', although previous careers included shuttle-maker and grocer. How they met is not known, although when the Hulme family were living in Southport, young Alice was a boarder at nearby Westlands School, so perhaps they met through the church there.
Sadly John and Alice had no children and were only married for four years when she died in March 1889 and was laid to rest near to baby Elizabeth Lever in Heaton Cemetery.

In September 1888 Elizabeth, William, and their six-month old son had moved to Thornton Manor in the Wirral village of Thornton Hough to be close to the new factory being built at Port Sunlight.
This large Victorian house, some twelve miles north of Chester, was rented from the family of its former occupant, a Liverpool merchant who had died four years earlier. This was their fifth home in fourteen years and was destined to become their main residence in the north of England.

It was here at Thornton Manor, two and a half years later, that Elizabeth, now 40, gave birth to their last child. Still-born, and once again un-named, their baby son was laid to rest alongside his sister in Bolton's Heaton Cemetery on their seventeenth wedding anniversary, April 15th 1891.

Thornton Manor in 1888

On Saturday August 23rd 1890, two years after moving to Thornton Manor, Elizabeth and William sailed from Liverpool with a large party of guests aboard the paddle steamer 'Mona's Isle' for a day out at Beaumaris in Anglesey to celebrate the completion of the first phase of the Port Sunlight factory.

Elizabeth, seen here in the middle of some of the Beaumaris party, is seated between William, his brother James, and James's wife, Annie.

Elizabeth and William Hulme, now aged 3, at Thornton Manor in 1891.

For the next few years, supported by his brother James, who by July 1889 had moved into nearby Thornton House, William concentrated on building and expanding the new factory and business at Port Sunlight. Any alterations to The Manor would have to wait. In fact there was some doubt as to whether they would even stay there, and in 1892 William had a new house built just down the road in the village of Thornton Hough. Possibly originally intended for their own occupation, it later became the home of his widowed father and sisters for a while.

On 18th April 1893 William finally bought Thornton Manor, and almost immediately set about altering it. Once more Elizabeth's home resounded to the sound of workmen. Alterations here were to be on such a grand scale that they even had to move out twice for long periods while work was completed.

Part of this time was spent travelling. After a six-week trip to America, they left in September 1895 for a four and a half month visit to Australia. It was actually more than eighteen months before they could return to live in The Manor.

Back from 'down-under' in February 1896, Elizabeth and William spent the next year shuttling between a house they were renting in Norfolk Street in London, Bridge Cottage in Port Sunlight, and his sisters' homes in Thornton Hough, before they finally moved back into The Manor in April 1897.

Bridge Cottage, sometimes referred to by William as 'Bridge House', was their home in Port Sunlight for several years. It was built on Park Road in late 1893 some six months after William had bought Thornton Manor. Beautifully finished throughout, Bridge Cottage was used by William and Elizabeth during 1896 and early 1897 while the alterations were being carried out at The Manor. It was also used occasionally by William when he needed to stay near to the factory.

Thornton Manor
as it appeared after completion of the the first major alterations. Elizabeth never lived to see later extensions which creating the house as it appears today.

William enjoyed driving his horse and carriage, seen here outside Bridge cottage with Elizabeth sitting alongside him on the driving seat.

Bridge Cottage Port Sunlight

In 1899, they were out of The Manor again, this time for eight months. They spent some of the time on a trip to the United States, some with friends and relations, and stayed in a rented property in Hoylake throughout the Autumn; but much of it was spent in yet another new home, Hillside, in Bolton.

Life at Thornton Manor

Thornton Manor was Elizabeth and William's Wirral home for nearly all their married lives, although they regularly shuttled to and fro between here and their other homes in Bolton and London.

Over the years, whenever they were in residence there always seemed to be plenty of visitors: children's parties, garden parties, visiting societies, and a constant stream of family, business and political guests.

William and Elizabeth greeting guests outside the front door of Thornton Manor.

Elizabeth and William are only just visible at the centre of this large group of visitors to Thornton Manor gardens.

Apparently very happy, William and Elizabeth totally surrounded by their young visitors by the lake.

William and Elizabeth with prime minister Asquith and guests during his visit in 1912.

Elizabeth, on the left, and William with two of their guests in the gardens. Elizabeth was often photographed wearing such very large hats.

Hanging on very tightly to the side of the boat, Elizabeth taking a trip on Thornton Manor lake.

After moving to Thornton Hough, Elizabeth and William continued to make frequent visits to Bolton. His mother and father, together with his unmarried sisters, were living in their home in Harwood. Elizabeth's brothers were both living *'on their own means'* in Sharples. John, 35 and now a widower, was living at 'Oaklea' in The Park, while brother James, 28 and still single, was being looked after by the same housekeeper, Margery Holland, at Spring Bank. Had their parents still been alive, presumably the sons would have both have been working for a living. However, following the death of their mother, they inherited the remainder of their late father's estate and as a result apparently no longer needed to work.

Every May, for many years, Elizabeth and William went to stay for the weekend with her cousin Walker Allen in Whitefield, near Bolton, where the Allen family owned large cotton mills and a dye works. Other times when visiting Bolton they regularly stayed with their close friends, Jonathan Simpson and his wife at their home 'Grey Gables'.

Jonathan Simpson

Lifelong friend of both Elizabeth and William since their days at the Misses Aspinwalls' School in Wood Street.

'Hillside', Bolton.

In February 1898 William finally bought another Bolton home, 'Hillside', *'to maintain a house in the Bolton area'*. Having it altered and enlarged took almost a year before they spent their first night there in February 1899. It then became their new home whilst yet more alteration work went on at Thornton Manor, and the servants were all relocated to Hillside complete with furniture and possessions. Three weeks later they left for a trip to America, and when they returned at the end of April, thankful to be back Elizabeth once again wrote in her journal *"Home sweet home"*.

Hillside was their main home throughout the Spring and Summer of 1899. They only returning to Thornton Manor in October after the alterations were complete.

They continued to use Hillside for weekend visits for the next two years until it was sold to William's widowed sister, Mrs Mary Tillotson, after William had yet another Bolton home built. This time it was on the side of Rivington Pike where he and Elizabeth had taken long walks when they were courting.

Their home at Rivington

In 1900 William bought the Rivington Estate to the west of Bolton and built a new home high up on Rivington Pike overlooking the Lancashire Plain. Known initially as 'Roynton Cottage', and later referred to simply as 'The Bungalow', Elizabeth wrote of the site selected for their new home as *".....a beautiful elevation and certainly a pretty scene to look down upon."*

The original building was a prefabricated wooden structure supplied by The Portable Building Company of Market Street, Manchester. It was delivered to nearby Horwich Station by train and then taken by horse and cart to the site where it was assembled.

'Roynton Cottage'

The original bunglaow at Rivington which was soon to be altered and extended like all their other homes.

Elizabeth and William first began using Roynton Cottage in January 1902, and they never stayed anywhere else after that when visiting the Bolton area.

Although more remote than their earlier Bolton houses, life here still continued for Elizabeth in the same way as it did in each of their other homes: visits to and from family members, daily letter writing, shopping expeditions, dinner parties, visits by various groups, and all the time William coming and going on his various business trips.

As in their other homes, there were alterations and additions to the property, and extensive landscaping taking place in the gardens on the hillside below.

This sundial, alongside the lawn below The Bungalow, is said to have been erected on the very spot where Elizabeth and William picnicked when courting.

Elizabeth greeting visitors at the entrance to the restored tithe barn which still stands in the public park that William created below The Bungalow grounds.

William and Elizabeth join the Boys' Brigade and Boy Scouts for church parade at their annual camp in The Bungalow grounds in 1910.

Their Rivington home was extensively altered and enlarged over a number of years.

On 8th July 1913, and by then known as 'The Bungalow', it was totally destroyed in an arson attack by a suffragette.

40-year old Edith Rigby was the wife of a Preston doctor. Her chauffeur drove her and a male sympathiser to Rivington where she set fire to the timber building using a keg of paraffin.

Edith Rigby

She was also responsible for planting a bomb in the Liverpool Corn Exchange and another arson attack at Blackburn Rovers Football Club.

Edith Rigby saw the destruction of The Bungalow as a protest against the government, which was ironic as William, by now a former Liberal member of parliament, was a supporter of women's suffrage. A typewritten note found near the scene said *"Lancashire's message to the King from the women: Votes for women due. Message to the King, Liverpool: Wake up the Government. First give us a reason to be loyal, and then try us."*

She is later quoted as saying *"I want to ask Sir William Lever whether he thinks his property on Rivington Pike is more valuable as one of his superfluous houses occasionally opened to people, or as a beacon lighted to King and Country to see here are some intolerable grievances for women."*

The fire was started while Elizabeth and William were guests at a dinner party given for the King and Queen by the Earl of Derby at his home in Knowsley near Liverpool. The news only reached them in the early hours of the following morning, after they had returned home to Thornton Manor.

Deeply saddened by the loss of their Bolton home, Elizabeth never lived to see The Bungalow rebuilt. She passed away just two weeks after it was destroyed.

Like their other homes, The Bungalow was filled with wonderful antiques and treasures, all of which were lost in the fire.

All that was left of the building after the fire were the brick chimneys and the iron roof trusses

Homes in London

With their Wirral and Bolton homes finally settled, it just remained to decide on their final London house. Over the years William spent a great deal of time at Lever Brothers' London office managing his ever-growing business. He travelled backwards and forwards between the different sites, sometimes several times a week. He often slept on the train to make maximum use of his time, but in all the time spent shuttling back and forth to the capital, Elizabeth slept on the train as little as possible, apparently preferring the comfort of her own bed.

During early trips to London William stayed at the National Liberal Club, but whenever Elizabeth was with him, they occupied suites at The Grand Hotel, and later The Park Lane Hotel.

During 1893 and 1894 they rented an apartment in Hyde Park Court, which later became the Hyde Park Hotel. They used the apartment exclusively while in London until their visit to America in October 1894.

Norfolk Street

In 1894 William had acquired the lease of 20, Norfolk Street, now called Dunraven Street, on the Grosvenor Mayfair Estate, just off Park Lane close to Marble Arch.

Although they only occupied the property for a few years, once again he carried out alterations and improvements to the interior. They moved out of Norfolk Street in September 1897 and for the next seven years, whenever they were in London they stayed in a suite of rooms either at The Grand Hotel, The Coburg Hotel in Grosvenor Square, or The Hyde Park Hotel at Albert Gate

Sydney Gross

They also began to spend weekends at Heath Lodge, the Hampstead home of Mr and Mrs Sydney Gross. Austrian by birth but American by nationality, Sydney Gross was managing the Kings Cross branch of The Benjamin Brook Company of Philadelphia.

The Benjamin Brook Co. was the manufacturer of Monkey Brand Soap, which Lever Brothers took over in January 1899. Sydney's wife Beatrice, a native of London who coincidentally shared a birthday with William, gave large dinner parties to which Elizabeth and William were regularly invited. Other guests included such notables as Mr Barratt of Pears Soap fame, and Sir Thomas Lipton, the well-known tea merchant.

Over the next seven years, although seventeen years her senior, Elizabeth became firm friends with Beatrice. They made frequent shopping trips into London as well as regular trips to the theatre, art galleries, and even one trip to the Henley Royal Regatta, although Elizabeth afterwards said that she was *"glad to have seen it but I don't desire to see it again."*

Heath Lodge's proximity to Eton, where young William Hulme began his studies in September 1901, was also an advantage and he too was a regular visitor. Father and son often rode out with Mr Gross on the Heath. In June 1902 Elizabeth wrote *"Coming so often, one begins to feel at home at Mrs Gross's "*.

But although she spent many enjoyable visits with Beatrice and Sydney Gross, in May 1904 she wrote *"I think I shall be glad when we have got our own home here for I am not fond of an unsettled life."*

Elizabeth and William began the search for a home for themselves soon after giving up Norfolk Street and they went to look at several houses in the area. One contender, Branch Hill Lodge *"certainly a most complete house except that there are no stables"*, was lost to a gentleman who was *'very anxious to possess it'*. The Whins, within walking distance of the Heath Lodge was another possibility, *"I feel that if spared to occupy it that it will be a very beautiful home"*. But in 1904 William purchased Hill House, or as it later became known, 'The Hill', right next door to the Gross's home.

William and Elizabeth seated on the terrace in the centre of a group of visitors at The Hill in 1909.

The Hill was a large mansion near the top of Hampstead Hill originally owned by the Hoare family, founders of England's oldest privately owned banking house. Having bought the house, the inevitable alterations followed. Outbuildings were pulled down and internal improvements made to the house *"which I fear is a very long way from being finished"*.

Housekeepers were interviewed in March 1905, but it was July before they were able to move in.

The Hill was now their base whenever they were in London. Garden parties, dinner parties and business meetings were held at the house. Visits were made to friends, and members of the family regularly came and went. There were trips into town for shopping and theatre visits, and in August 1908 Elizabeth made her first trip on 'The Tube' when she visited the Franco-British Exhibition at White City. If they were there on a Sunday they would attend one of the local churches, and she spent a great deal of time keeping up with her correspondence.

Their Hampstead home also provided a useful base for William when he was attending the House of Commons. After standing as a Liberal Party candidate on several occasions, he was finally elected as Member of Parliament for Wirral in January 1906 and served four years in the government.

The Hill after the original alterations to the house and gardens.

The Hill, now in multiple occupancy, as it appears today.

The rest of the family

Not long after beginning work on the factory and housing at Port Sunlight, William had bought large areas of land around their home at Thornton Manor, including much of the village of Thornton Hough. Old thatched properties were demolished and, using the same architects responsible for Port Sunlight, new cottages were built for his rural tenants and workers.

Several larger properties were also built in the village and, while Elizabeth and William were moving and re-organising their various homes, most of the extended Lever family had moved to Thornton Hough. Whenever she was there, Elizabeth's social life was filled with a wealth of family visits and gatherings, frequent dinners and house parties at Thornton Manor, as well as the constant round of formal engagements with her husband.

William's sisters, Emily, Alice, and Harriette, together with their widowed father, had moved from Bolton to Thornton Hough in May 1894. In August that same year his other sister Jane and her husband, John Ferguson, moved into Thornton Lodge just down the road on the other side of the village, and in September 1895, William's widowed sister Eliza Bromiley also moved from Bolton to the village.

Elizabeth's two brothers had stayed in Bolton where John too now had a housekeeper, Elizabeth Wilson, who was to stay with him for many years to come.

Her brother James died aged just 41 in April 1904 at Elizabeth and William's hilltop home 'The Bungalow' and, following a short service there, he was buried in the same grave as his sister-in-law, Alice, at Heaton Cemetery.
That evening Elizabeth Ellen wrote *'Alas I only have one brother now.'* Now the sole surviving members of the Hulme family after James' death, Elizabeth and John regularly kept in touch.

In 1911 Elizabeth's brother, John, was still living at 61 Sharples Park, Bolton with his housekeeper and was destined to outlive all the other members of the family. He died aged 80 in January 1935 and was buried three days later with his wife and brother in the Hulme family grave at Heaton Cemetery, Bolton.

The grave of Elizabeth's brothers James and John, and John's wife Alice, in Heaton Cemetery, Bolton is now marked by a pink granite headstone. It was apparently erected after John's death by William Hulme Lever, who was by then the 2nd Lord Leverhulme.

With John and James both childless, John's death brought the Hulme name to an end. Today it is still preserved in the name of Hulme Hall in Port Sunlight, and of course in the 'Leverhulme' title.

William was made a baronet on 6th July 1911 in the coronation honours for King George V.
Elizabeth became Lady Lever but never lived to enjoy the status as the wife of a peer of the realm. She died four years before her husband received his first peerage in 1917 as Baron Leverhulme of Bolton-le-Moors. Created by William in 1917, the title combined his own family name with Elizabeth's and is an enduring tribute to her memory.
She was never Lady Leverhulme, which is why the art gallery and museum in Port Sunlight dedicated to her memory is known as 'The Lady Lever' Gallery.

But this was not the only honour that Elizabeth received.

Considering the amount written about William's trips around the globe, and later their son's various expeditions, with the exception of her last trip there is remarkably little recorded of Elizabeth's travels.

Two years after she became Lady Lever, in 1913, she was elected a Fellow of the Royal Geographical Society in recognition of the extensive world travel she undertook in the company of her husband. Sadly she was only able to enjoy this new honour for three months before she passed away.

William himself had been a Fellow of the Society since 1902, but on April 29th 1913, Lady Elizabeth Ellen Lever was elected a Fellow in her own right. Usually there was no ceremony to mark the event. Fellows of the Society were elected in batches of up to twenty or more. A formal mention would be made in the agenda at a suitable meeting, the list of names was published in the next edition of the Journal, and new Fellows received a copy of their election certificate in the post. However, Elizabeth attended a presentation on May 7th and found it a bit of an ordeal although she felt '*it was a success as far as not disgracing myself*'.

Her election followed a long debate which had extended over twenty years on whether or not women should be admitted to The Society. Elizabeth was among the first women to be elected as Fellows. She was one of several who were honoured in this way. She was proposed by Lord Curzon, the first Marquess of Kedleston, who as President of the Society had championed the vote to admit women. Her seconder was Douglas Freshfield, the renowned climber, explorer, and Honorary Secretary of the Society for many years.

Throughout her life Elizabeth had travelled a great deal around Britain, commuting frequently between their various residences in the north of England and their homes in London.

There were also regular holidays in the early part of the marriage. Each year, if not abroad, some part of late Summer or Autumn was spent in different parts of the United Kingdom - Wales, Ireland, Scotland, and the Lake District were all visited, as well as Yorkshire and the south coast.

But, considering the difficulties of foreign travel at that time, the list of her foreign trips is quite remarkable.

Between 1891 and her death in 1913, Elizabeth went many times to Europe and America.

She visited Africa and Australia, sailed across the Atlantic fourteen times and round the world twice – in opposite directions.

In all Elizabeth made a total of twenty trips abroad, some short, some lasting as long as six months, but never alone, always with William. There were no quick transatlantic flights or high speed trains, and this was long before the age of cruise ships. Vessels did not have stabilisers, and passages were often rough. There was no air-conditioning, and temperatures could vary from bitterly cold in the southern oceans to searing heat in the heart of Africa.

On most of his trips William combined business with pleasure at each place they visited. He took the opportunity to pursue his various business interests, and sometimes left Elizabeth and the rest of the party to fend for themselves for days on end.

A Holiday in Egypt

William and Elizabeth's first major trip abroad together was in fact a holiday - to North Africa. With the new soap business firmly established at Port Sunlight and needing a rest, in 1891 they went to Egypt.

Young William was left at home in care of his nurse and their housekeeper, Miss Clara Green, who was to play a significant role in the family's life for the next thirty years.

William Hulme with Clara Green, their housekeeper.

Setting off on December 1st from London, Elizabeth and William travelled first to Paris and then overland via Nice to Marseilles. There they joined the steamer 'Senegal' to take them across the Mediterranean to the port of Alexandria on the North African coast. After travelling by train to Cairo they boarded a paddle steamer, the 'Memphis', for a cruise down the Nile.

Life on board a Nile cruiser in those days would have been very different.

Over the next fortnight they visited various wonderful sights including the tombs of Ben Hassen, the city of Luxor, and the island of Philae, although Elizabeth said that the constant vibration of the boat *'took a good deal from the pleasure of the voyage'.*

Pictures of Elizabeth taken during her trip to Egypt with William in 1891.

Retracing their steps through Cairo and Alexandria, they sailed back to Brindisi on the 'Enterpe' and, after a long train trip via Rome and Paris to London, they finally arrived back at Thornton Manor on January 14th 1892.

Nine months later Elizabeth and William set off again. This time on a round-the-world trip, taking their 4½-year old son with them, together with Clara, who was now his governess. It meant they would spend their second successive Christmas away from home.

The four of them set sail for America from Liverpool on September 14th 1892 on the steamship Germanic. Over a hundred friends and relations gathered to see them off.

Elizabeth, Clara, and William Hulme on board ship during their round-the-world trip.

William kept a detailed diary of their journey. His account of the trip was later published - first in instalments in the local paper, The Birkenhead News, and later as a book entitled *"Following the Flag. Jottings of a Jaunt round the World."*

Remarkably William never once mentions his wife or son in the whole of the narrative of their six-month long trip.

Clara also kept a diary of their trip which she wrote for the benefit of her mother to give her *"a taste of the world outside her home where she so peacefully spends the evening of her life."*

SS Australia

The vessel which carried the party across the Pacific and then back to England.

After a sometimes uncomfortable nine-day voyage they landed at New York. They spent three days in the city before travelling by train to Canada where they visited Montreal, Toronto, St Johns, and the spectacular Niagara Falls.

William, Elizabeth, William Hulme, and Clara wrapped in waterproofs, photographed against the backdrop of Niagara Falls.

They returned via Chicago and Salt Lake City to San Francisco where they boarded the recently commissioned SS Australia to sail across the Pacific in late October, six weeks after leaving England.

First they went to Honolulu and Hawaii, where they sailed out to see the Kilauea volcano, and then on the SS Manposa to Auckland and Wellington in New Zealand where they spent Christmas that year. New Year was celebrated aboard the SS Manarapu en-route to Tasmania and Melbourne. After a month travelling around Australia by train, they rejoined the SS Australia at Adelaide and on February 1st 1893 set sail for home via The Suez Canal, Malta and Gibraltar.

After five and half weeks at sea, they landed at Plymouth on March 9th and went by train straight to Thornton Manor, arriving back 177 days after leaving home and travelling more than 30,000 miles. The journey would have been considerably longer had it not been for the Suez Canal which had opened twenty four years earlier.

Elizabeth joined William on two trips in 1895. In March they sailed from Liverpool for America on the SS Majestic, and once again they were seen off by a large group of friends.

This time the party consisted of Elizabeth and William, their son who celebrated his 7th birthday during the crossing, and William's sister and her husband, Mary and William Tillotson. They were also accompanied by Miss Ada Walmsley, who was young William's governess for this particular voyage, and a Mr Jowett, Mr Lever's 20-year old correspondence clerk.

William and Elizabeth aboard ship.

Arriving in New York after a fairly rough crossing, they stayed at the Majestic Hotel on 72nd Street and 8th Avenue. There they had a suite of room consisting of four bedrooms and a sitting room, costing the princely sum of $180 per week for 'five adults and a boy' including full board.

The Majestic Hotel in New York.

After a week in New York, they set off to travel south but went to the wrong station and missed the train, so they then had to wait until the next day to start their two-day journey to Vicksburgh. The ladies *occupied the parlour in the car and found it very comfortable* and Elizabeth indulged in some knitting to pass the time.

Following four days of business at the Oil Mills in Vicksburgh they boarded the sternwheel paddleship 'Natchez' to sail down the Mississippi to Baton Rouge from where they caught the train for New Orleans.

'Natchez' The Mississippi Steamboat.

After yet more business meetings in New Orleans, they went on by train to Houston, Texas. The return trip by train to New York via New Orleans, Vicksburgh and Chattanooga was made even longer by a fatal rail accident on their route. Elizabeth then stayed in New York while William went off again on business to Canada where he spent a few days. They all eventually left New York aboard the SS Majestic for Liverpool arriving back at the end of May.

The White Star Line's SS Majestic.

Just four months later they were off on their travels yet again, and once more to Australia, not round the world this time but going around South Africa on the way out, and then back via the Suez Canal.

For the third time in five years, Elizabeth and William would celebrate Christmas far from home.

They sailed from Southampton on September 21st 1895 aboard the SS Tantallon Castle, with seven year-old William being looked after this time by another new governess, a Miss Coates. They were accompanied once again by Clara Green, now Lady Lever's 'companion', and by William's widowed sister, Eliza Bromiley.

Apparently not entirely satisfied with their accommodation, Elizabeth wrote *"The Tantallon Castle does not compare favourably with other vessels we have travelled on"*.

After stopping briefly at Madeira they landed at Cape Town on October 8th. Leaving the rest of the party to their own devices, William, accompanied by his sister Eliza, went to Kimberley for a fortnight on business, before the whole party sailed on the RMS Ionic for Australia. The ten-day voyage through the southern oceans to Hobart was at times very cold. It snowed, and one day they even encountered an iceberg. What a contrast Australia must have seemed when they got there, with temperatures as high as 92°F degrees in the shade.

The Balmain Factory, Australia.

It was during this visit that, on December 27th 1895, Elizabeth carried out one of her ceremonial duties by cutting the first sod for the new oil mill at the Lever Brothers' Australian factory in Balmain, a suburb of Sidney.

It was also whilst they were there that they received news that William's brother, James, was very ill. Communications then were remarkably good. They received telegrams when on land and 'marconigrams' on board ship, but getting back from Australia in the days before air travel was a slow process. Cutting short their trip, they abandoned a planned visit to India and sailed straight home on the 'Oceania' on which they saw in the New Year.

The news they received of James was no better when they called in at Albany and Colombo, so after they had sailed through the Suez Canal, William left the vessel at Brindisi and travelled home overland to Wirral to see him. Elizabeth and the others sailed on to England where they arrived on February 7th 1896, and then they too hurried home to find out how James was.

James Darcy Lever

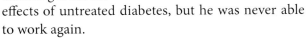

James was very poorly and there were serious concerns about his health and even his mental state. He was eventually diagnosed as suffering from the effects of untreated diabetes, but he was never able to work again.

No longer involved with the business to which he had given his name, he officially retired from Lever Brothers in February 1898, after which he spent most of his life at his home in Thornton Hough where he passed away in March 1910.

Despite all her travelling, Elizabeth always liked to return home….. *"Home sweet home"*……a sentiment she often repeated on arriving at whichever of their various houses it happened to be at the end of a long journey…….. and whenever she was at home, she was often involved in some local event or another.

On the steps at Bromborough Golf Club with Gladys Ravenscroft, later to become British Ladies Amateur Champion

With a group of other guests at a ball in Port Sunlight

In 1894 William went to America again, but this time Elizabeth decided she preferred to stay at home, so he took his sisters Emily Bromiley and Jane Ferguson with him.

William and Elizabeth soon resumed their travels together. Two weeks in Ireland and a weekend in Scotland in 1896 were followed by another six-week business trip to America and Canada later that year. They were back in plenty of time for Christmas which was spent at Hesketh Grange in Thornton Hough with William's father and sisters because work on the alterations was still on-going at Thornton Manor. After being reinstalled at The Manor the following April, they then spent every Christmas there for the next fifteen years.

Two short business trips to Europe in 1897 and 1898 with William were followed by a holiday at Ullswater in 1898.

It was not exactly an intimate holiday for two; twenty six of them went to stay for nearly four weeks at the Sun Hotel at Pooley Bridge. The party included their son William Hulme and his cousin James Darcy junior, William's sister Mrs Mary Tillotson, sister-in-law Mrs Annie Lever, companion Clara Green, best friend Jonathan Simpson, and various other members of the Lever family.

There were many trips and outings on the lake, and although there were a lot of them there, on the 23rd August Elizabeth wrote *"Will said today was one of the happiest he had had for many years."* but she must have been glad when it was coming to an end - *"Our last day, I feel rejoiced to say."*

Another six-week visit to America and Canada in 1899 was followed in the Autumn by a stay 'at the seaside' in a house they rented at Hoylake for six weeks.

In 1901 they spent two weeks in the late Summer at The Crown Hotel in Harrogate. Although they treated it as a holiday, going out for many drives, visiting Harewood House, Ripon Cathedral etc., the trip was also for the benefit of William's health. He was suffering from rheumatic gout which was being treated with massage, baths, a strict diet and the obligatory 'taking the waters'.

The Crown Hotel, Harrogate.

Four weeks later, on September 12th 1901, as their son William Hulme was starting his new life at Eton they were off round the world again, this time in the opposite direction.

Not quite 'around the world in eighty days' the trip lasted 94 days, but that was remarkably quick considering that they visited Australia, New Zealand, Canada and America en-route, and once again William had business meetings and visits to the company's establishments in all the various countries.

The party, which included William's sister, Harriette, and his 24-year old niece Ella Tillotson, went first overland to Marseilles where they picked up the SS India. Having sailed through the Suez Canal they stopped briefly in late September at Colombo in former Ceylon after a rather rough voyage across the Indian Ocean. Then they went on to Adelaide, where they arrived on October 12th, before travelling overland to Sydney.

Elizabeth, Harriette, and Ella remained in the city for a fortnight while William visited Queensland on company business. Leaving Sydney on the SS Sierra they sailed to America via Auckland and Samoa. After landing at San Francisco, the party crossed North America by train by a circuitous route calling at Colorado, Missouri, Illinois, Toronto, Boston, and finally New York.

They sailed home on the SS Oceanic, arriving back in Liverpool in time for Christmas at The Manor, and the annual New Year gathering of Port Sunlight employees.

There were no foreign trips in 1902, the year that Elizabeth took her last proper holiday. With William away in America, accompanied by son William, nephew James Darcy, Clara Green, and Davies, their groom, she stayed for ten days in August at The Alexandra Hotel in Oban on the west coast of Scotland.

Apart from a few odd weekends away, William and Elizabeth never took another proper holiday together for the rest of their married lives. There were, however, a few more foreign trips, and Elizabeth always took the opportunity to visit places of interest wherever they stayed.

A week in Europe and two more trips to America during February and August 1904, gave her plenty of opportunity to do some sightseeing. There was quite a group on the second transatlantic trip: William and Elizabeth, her maid Cecilia Dulston, their son William Hulme, as well as James Lever Ferguson, James Darcy Lever junior, and Jim Simpson.

Although William was still regularly off on his travels, it was to be five years before Elizabeth herself ventured abroad again with him. A brief visit to Paris in October 1909, and ten days in Holland and France in early 1910, were followed by a remarkably quick visit to North America in November of the same year. In what was described as a 'weekend visit', they travelled there and back in just over a fortnight aboard The Mauretania. and were back home before some people even realised they had been away.

Launched in 1907, The Mauretania was the fastest transatlantic liner for more than twenty years, cutting the journey time to New York by a third.

Compared with earlier trips on the older, slower liners this must have been a totally new experience. Another passenger at the time wrote "This ship is like a palace, it is really wonderful. Everything is so comfortable and no motion to speak of."

At the beginning of 1912 Elizabeth, now Lady Lever, set out with William on the first of two trips that year to Africa. On January 6th they left Southampton aboard the RMS Armadale Castle bound for South Africa. Once again Elizabeth's maid, Dulston, from Thornton Manor went with them.

RMS Armadale Castle

Arriving in Cape Town after a three-week voyage the party went by train, first to Kimberley and Johannesburg, and then on to Durban where the previous year Lever Brothers had opened their first South African factory. There they joined the employees and their families at the annual picnic, and after tea Elizabeth presented the sports prizes.

Returning to Capetown, Elizabeth once again performed that ceremony of 'cutting the first sod'. This time it was for the company's new Woodstock works at Salt River, but it was in marked contrast to the ceremony at Port Sunlight twenty four years earlier. With just three local boys looking on, she loosened a piece of ground using a penknife - *because there was nothing else available.*

After just ten days in the country they re-boarded the Armadale Castle for the trip back to Southampton, arriving back in late February.

On April 15th that year The Titanic sank en-route to New York after striking an iceberg. This must have been extremely significant for anyone involved in so much transatlantic travel as William. Coincidentally, Geoffrey Barnes, the son of Elizabeth's Wigan doctor, was 4th Officer on the Carpathia which was involved in the rescue of Titanic survivors.

In April Elizabeth and William went to their son's wedding in Manchester. William Hulme was the apple of Elizabeth's eye and she was very proud of him. Before leaving home for the wedding he had given her a sprig of forget-me-not.

She felt sure that his fiancée, Marion Beatrice Bryce-Smith, the younger daughter of Bryce Smith from Walley near Manchester, would make him very happy and would be a good wife to him.

Marion and William Hulme

They were married at St.Clements New Church in the Parish of Chorlton-cum-Hardy, and they made a beautiful couple. Had she still been alive, Elizabeth would have been very sad when their marriage came to an end some twenty years later.

Elizabeth, seated on the right, with William at the wedding of their son and Marion Bryce-Smtih on 24th April 1912.

After seeing them off on their honeymoon, Elizabeth and William went straight to London to prepare for a brief trip to Europe which included various business dinners and meetings in France and Germany.

In late June 1912 Elizabeth and William led the Sunday School Anniversary procession through Port Sunlight village. Concerned that their formal titles of Sir William and Lady Lever would appear rather daunting to the village children, they had agreed to be known by them as 'Uncle and Auntie Lever'.

In July William and Elizabeth hosted a visit by Herbert Asquith, the Liberal prime minister, to Port Sunlight and Thornton Manor.

Uncle & Auntie Lever

Sir William and Lady Elizabeth leading the Sunday School Anniversary procession through Port Sunlight village.

The Children's Song
to
"Auntie Lever."

December has come round again
With all its joys and pleasures :
The children's dance, the Christmas tree
Laden with precious treasures.
And there is one day in this month—
A very happy mirthday—
So bright, and full of joy, for that
Is "Auntie Lever's" birthday.

So, Auntie dear, we want to tell
You of our love and gladness ;
To wish you health—a long, long life
For ever free from sadness.
And more than this—a sweet, sweet thought
That time must never sever,
That you love us and we love you,
And we shall love you ever.

Port Sunlight,
December 4th, 1911.

This special song had been composed and performed by the Port Sunlight children to celebrate Elizabeth's 60th birthday the previous year

Surrounded by hundreds of supporters there to greet Prime Minister Asquith, Elizabeth is almost hidden behind the flag-draped table outside Thornton Manor as William addresses the crowd.

At the end of July once again Elizabeth welcomed hundreds of children to the annual Thornton Manor picnic, an event which always gave her immense pleasure.

The children's annual picnic at Thornton Manor in 1912

The trip to the Congo

In November 1912 Sir William and Lady Lever set out on what turned out to be Elizabeth's last major foreign trip, and certainly the most arduous.

The previous year William had entered into an agreement with the Belgian Government to cultivate and collect palm fruit in the Congo. So accompanied by Elizabeth, her maid Dulston and a *'group of thoroughly experienced gentlemen of wide knowledge of tropical affairs',* they set out to visit their new territory.

An article in one of the local magazines, The African World, reported that Lady Lever's *"determination to accompany her husband throws a sidelight which eloquently reveals an unselfish and courageous devotion."*

The SS Leopoldville which carried Elizabeth, William, and the rest of their party on the 5000 mile journey to and from the Congo.

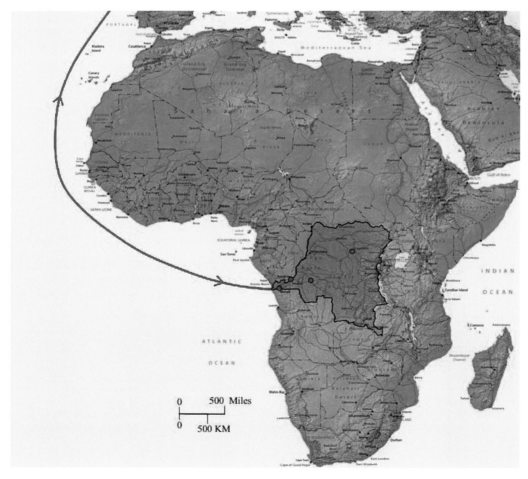

In November 1912, after travelling via Dover, Ostend, and Brussels to Antwerp, they set sail aboard the SS Leopoldville for Africa. By wireless telegram William responded to the good luck messages from Port Sunlight with *"Weather calm. Spirits and health are excellent for self and all party"*.

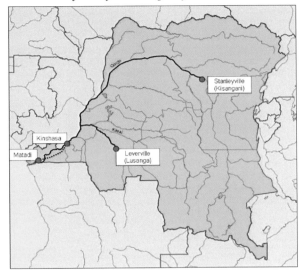

The route of their trip through The Congo.

Three and a half weeks later on December 7th they arrived at Matadi, Congo's main seaport, situated on the Congo River ninety two miles from its mouth. Beyond Matadi the rapids make the river impassable for a long stretch, so the party then travelled overland by train, first to Thysville, now called Mbanza-Ngungu, and then to Kinshasa where they boarded a river steamer, the SS Lusanga, which was to be their home for the next two months.

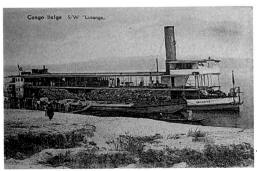

The SS Lusanga

**Elizabeth aboard the river steamer
SS Lusanga.**

From Kinshasa they went first to visit Leverville, the settlement that had been adopted and named by the company as the centre of its palm oil extracting operations, and is now known as Lusanga.

At that time there were no real roads and the only way to travel through the dense jungle was by boat along the rivers. It was a long way and it took two and a half weeks to get there. First they had to sail part-way up the Congo and then travel east via the Kasai and Kwilu Rivers until they arrived at Leverville.

Leverville

They had hoped to be at Leverville by Christmas, but as a result of repeated delays for refuelling with wood, they had to spend it on the river – although they were pleasantly surprised to receive Christmas letters for them from friends and family which had been secretly entrusted to Elizabeth's maid, Dulston, before they left England.

They arrived at Leverville just two days after Christmas and, considering the distance they had come, they spent a remarkably short time there. After four very busy days they were on their way once again.

During this part of the trip, Elizabeth rescued a five-year old native girl who had been sold into slavery by her parents in one of the villages they visited. Taking her with them, they left her in the care of a Jesuit Mission Station on their way back down river.

Elizabeth with the young native girl she rescued during their trip in the Congo.

Retracing their route to the main Congo river they now turned north and headed upstream for Stanleyville, originally named after William Stanley the famous English explorer, but now renamed Kisangani. They reached Stanleyville on January 26th. Again they stayed for just two days before heading back downstream. The trip back took only two weeks, presumably because they were travelling much faster with the current.

Dense jungle stretched for miles either side of the Congo river.

While William made various visits ashore along the route for business and pleasure, they collected a veritable menagerie of animals: first a gift from a Mr Mingles of a monkey which Elizabeth decided to call Jill *'hoping to get a Jack later'*; then a handsome dog called Tiger which was once the property of an elephant hunter called Mr. Jordan; then a black monkey she called Jack, from a Monsieur French, and a baby monkey she named Kilty; two more that were not given names, and finally a chimpanzee from a Mr Horn.

The dog Tiger was clearly a great favourite and started sneaking into their cabin to sleep, while the poor monkeys were all given a bath which Elizabeth hoped *"in consequence are feeling better."*

During the trip through the Central Africa jungle they crossed the equator four times and travelled over 7,000 miles in day-time temperatures that were regularly in excess of ninety degrees in the shade.

Arriving back at Kinshasa in mid-February, they finally left the SS Lusanga which had been their home for two months, and travelled to Thysville. At two and a half thousand feet above sea-level it was much cooler there, Elizabeth even felt that *"a fire would be welcome this evening."* It was also decided that it was too cold in England to take the monkeys back straight away, so they would remain in Kinshasa and be brought back the following April.

- which apparently they were, because by the May at least one was safely installed at Thornton Manor, although their ultimate fate is not known.

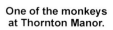

One of the monkeys at Thornton Manor.

After a sometimes monotonous three-week return trip by sea of nearly 5,000 miles aboard the SS Leopoldville, William, Elizabeth, and her maid, Dulston, finally arrived back at Thornton Manor on March 11th.

The next day there was the first of a whole series of 'Welcome Home' events: a staff reception, a Village Children's Welcome, and a Sunday School thanksgiving service, all in the Auditorium at Port Sunlight, followed by a special service in Christ Church.

Lady Lever and Sir William were greeted by enthusiastic crowds on their return to Port Sunlight.

Lady Lever and Sir William apparently in good health and pleased to be back from their long trip to Africa.

Being welcomed back by factory and office staff awaiting them in the Auditorium.

The scene inside the Auditorium.

Demolished in 1938, the Auditorium, which originally stood in The Dell in the centre of Port Sunlight village, was used over the years for many of the special events that Elizabeth and William attended.

Ceremonial Occasions

During her lifetime, Elizabeth was called upon to accompany William to numerous luncheons and dinners, even dining with royalty. She was no stranger to such celebrations and occasions which she seems to have embraced as part of her role as the wife of her ever pioneering husband.

They also performed a variety of ceremonial functions, some of which she carried out herself - usually with, but sometimes without, William.

Her first major event had undoubtedly been the cutting of that first sod to mark the start of work on the Port Sunlight factory in March 1888. Thereafter, she repeated the same ceremony in both Australia in 1895, and South Africa in 1912.

In this country Elizabeth officially laid numerous foundation stones, and declared a whole variety of buildings, bazaars and garden parties, 'duly open' – all of which resulted in a considerable collection of ceremonial keys, trowels, spades and gavels which are now in the keeping of various private and public archives and museums.

She laid her first foundation stone in September 1900 at the Dean Congregational Mission in Bolton, and in December she officially opened the nearby Congregational Church on Chorley Old Road with a golden key.

Some of the ceremonial golden keys presented to Elizabeth when she opened various schools, churches and public parks.

Eighteen months later in June 1902 Elizabeth lit the local Coronation Bonfire by electrical remote control. The following day she opened an extension to Pennant House Grounds near to the Port Sunlight village with another golden key, and then planted an oak tree which is still there today.

Elizabeth formally opening the gates to the extension to the public grounds at Pennant House near to the Port Sunlight factory.

Then, using a spade wrapped with ribbon, and surrounded by a large crowd of dignatories and onlookers, Elizabeth planted an oak tree in the grounds.

In April 1903 she laid the foundation stone of the new school of Edgworth Congregational Church near Bolton saying *"Friends, I have great pleasure in declaring this stone well and truly laid and in wishing you every success in your good work."*

…..and as a complete contrast she opened the Port Sunlight miniature rifle range by firing the first shot, whilst William was away on business.

On September 30th 1902 Elizabeth laid the foundation stone of Christ Church Port Sunlight, the first of two churches built on Wirral by William.

Elizabeth, second from the right, on the platform with William and the various other dignatories at the laying ceremony.

Presented with a ceremonial gavel and trowel to mark the occassion, she said .....

"Thank you for the opportunity you have so kindly given me of laying this stone. The village could never be complete without this church for divine worship and in declaring this stone well and truly laid, I hope to venture for Christ Church Port Sunlight a long and useful career as a centre of religious life in the village."

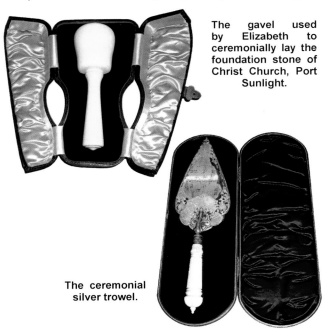

The gavel used by Elizabeth to ceremonially lay the foundation stone of Christ Church, Port Sunlight.

The ceremonial silver trowel.

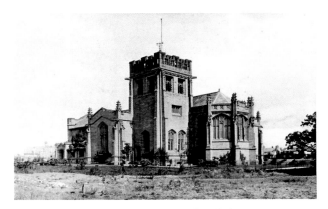

Christ Church, Port Sunlight.

The foundation stone was laid with the inscription facing into the church, apparently in anticipation of the later building of the family tomb.

Christ Church, Port Sunlight.
Laying of the Foundation Stone
by Mrs. W. H. LEVER.
Tuesday, 30th September, 1902.
Seat No. 433
TO BE RETAINED BY THE VISITOR.

Attendance at the laying ceremony was by ticket only.

Twenty months later, with building work complete, in the evening of June 8th 1904 Elizabeth symbolically turned yet another golden key to open Christ Church and said *"I hope sincerely that to everyone concerned this church may be the means of great good both now and in the future."*

The golden key presented to Elizabeth to perform the opening ceremony.

St George's, Thornton Hough

On April 11th 1906, almost four years after laying the foundation stone of Christ Church, Elizabeth laid the foundation stone of William's second new church, this time in Thornton Hough, describing it as *"our little Norman church here to be called St George's Congregational Church"*.

A large crowd was in attendance when Elizabeth laid the foundation stone at St George's Church in the centre of Thornton Hough.

The ceremony was followed by '*an old fashioned tea party of bygone days*'. The architect, James Lomax Simpson, who was the son of their life-long friend Jonathan Simpson, then presented Elizabeth with this rather large gavel, together with a beautiful silver inkstand instead of a trowel.

St George's Church, Thornton Hough.

Just over a year later, on May 29th 1907 Elizabeth formally opened St George's, although William didn't get back to join her until the ceremony was over. Once more she received another beautiful key as a memento of the occasion.

Elizabeth, accompanied by the Minister of St. George's, and followed by a crowd of villagers, making her way to officially open the church at Thornton Hough.

The gavel used by Elizabeth when she laid the foundation stone of St George's in Thornton Hough.

This golden key was presented to Elizabeth when she opened St. George's Church.

Apart from laying the foundation stone of St. George's Church in April, Elizabeth carrried out several other ceremonies during 1906.

In February that year, three weeks after William was elected MP for Wirral, she had officially opened the Hoylake and West Kirby Cottage Hospital.

Hoylake Congregational Church, opened by Elizabeth on 18th May 1906.

In May she opened the Congregational Church at Hoylake, followed a month later in June by the Moreton Presbyterian Church. In September she laid the foundation stone of the new schools at the Seacombe Primitive Methodist Church where this time she was presented with a silver salver.

Some of the many ceremonial trowels presented to Elizabeth when she laid various foundation stones in Wirral and in Bolton.

Prenton Congregational Church

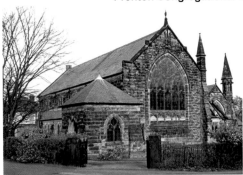

In June 1908 Elizabeth laid the Foundation Stone of the New Congregational Church at Prenton in Birkenhead, and two weeks later another foundation stone – one of seven stones for the New Wesleyan Church and Schools at Neston, on her own once again as William was away.

The official party at the laying of the foundations stones of Neston Weslyan Church, 27th June 1908.

In August 1910 Elizabeth even launched a ship - the SS Kulambangra at Old Kilpatrick in Scotland.

The SS Kulambangra launched by Elizabeth on August 25th 1910.

The last weeks of Elizabeth's life

Elizabeth and William spoke highly of the climate during their travels in the Congo and are reported as having enjoyed excellent health – which appears to contradict suggestions that Elizabeth's death was due to a chill contracted during her trip.

Given the length of time between her return and her death four and half months later, this seems unlikely. It is more probable that it was a combination of tiredness from doing so much travelling, the shock of the burning down of their home at Rivington, and a little too much sun at a garden party the previous weekend, which may have caused the chill which led to her demise. She apparently felt perfectly well until just a few days before she passed away.

Between their return and mid-May they spent a great deal of time travelling to their various homes at Thornton Manor, The Bungalow, and The Hill, before they left for a week's trip to Europe on May 10th. After their return they again spent time at the three houses and attended several events including two garden parties at The Manor and dinner with the King and Queen at Knowsley on the 7th July, the same night that The Bungalow was destroyed.

Elizabeth, accompanied by William, talking to guests at a garden party at Thornton Manor on July 5th, less than three weeks befor she died.

Three days later they attended the visit by the King and Queen to Bolton, and then they went to see the devastation at their Rivington home which had been completely destroyed by the fire. Sadly Elizabeth would never live to see The Bungalow rebuilt.

After returning to Thornton Hough they went to Hampstead, then back again to The Manor from where William left for a trip to Paris on the 19th after attending a garden party at their son and daughter-in-law's home at Heathfield in nearby Bebington. Lady Lever recorded that day that she *"found it quite hot and the number there a little bewildering."*

The following day, Sunday July 20th, she wrote in her journal *"I am feeling just a wee bit seedy this morning. I must try to continue my trust and hope in all things I may be led right"* – that was the last entry she ever made in her journals which she had faithfully written every day since 1897 – journals in which she often questioned her own worthiness, but always put her trust in God.

That Sunday, William Hulme wrote to his father who was away in Europe on business, '*.. mother not been very well today…doctor says there is absolutely nothing to worry about. Slight congestion in one lung but that in two or three days hopes she will be well again….been very tired last week or two especially the week of the King's visit…only Miss Green and Dulston there.*'

Elizabeth's chill had turned into pneumonia, and William hurried back from the continent to be at his wife's side. She died at Thornton Manor on Thursday 24th July 1913 after just four day's illness.

Elizabeth's death certificate

224	Twenty fourth July 1913. Thornton Manor Thornton Hough R.D.	Elizabeth Ellen Lever	Female	62 Years	Wife of Sir William Hesketh Lever Baronet.	Acute Croupous Pneumonia Syncope. Certified by Andrew Bassett Brown M.D.	W Hulme Lever Son Present at the death Heathfield Bebington	Twenty fourth July 1913	W Roberts Registrar.

Elizabeth's death certificate, signed by local doctor Andrew Cassels-Brown MD, records that she died of acute croupus pneumonia. Sometimes called 'ordinary pneumonia', this is an acute infection characterized by sudden onset of a chill, high fever, rapid progression, and sudden decline.

There is no evidence whatsoever, as has been suggested by some, that the outdoor bedroom at Thornton Manor played any part in Elizabeth's death, or that she ever even slept there.
Sleeping outside was a habit apparently adopted by William only after her death. In all probability she died in the warmth of her own bedroom. She passed away a few minutes after midnight with William and their son at her bedside.

Messages of condolence came from around the world, from local people, and from many individuals Elizabeth had met on her travels, including the King and Queen with whom she and William had dined less three weeks earlier.

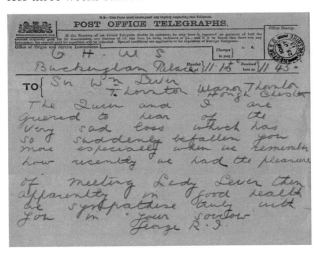

**The telegram from The King
to Sir William Lever at The Manor, Thornton Hough, Cheshire,
received via Neston Sub Post Office on July 25th 1913.**

**"The Queen and I are grieved to hear of the very sad loss
which has so suddenly befallen you. More especially when
we remember how recently we had the pleasure of meeting
Lady Lever then apparently in good health. We sympathise
truly with you in your sorrow.   George R.I**

Elizabeth's funeral took place just two days later on Saturday 26th July 1913. After a private service for the family and staff at Thornton Manor, a public service was held at Christ Church, Port Sunlight - the church where she had laid the foundation stone eleven years earlier.

On the day of the funeral the church was crowded with family members, local dignitaries, and representatives of numerous organisations, together with company employees from far and wide.

**So many people wanted to attend Elizabeth's funeral
that entry into the church was by ticket only. Hundreds
more stood outside.**

In the graveyard were members of the village's various uniformed organisations paying their respects, including the National Reserve, the Port Sunlight Ambulance Brigade, and the Port Sunlight Boys' Brigade who lined the pathway to the grave.

**Port Sunlight Boys' Brigade lining the path to the
grave at the funeral of Elizabeth, Lady Lever.**

Elizabeth's final resting place

In this view of the church yard, taken during Elizabeth's funeral, the pall bearers can just be seen carrying her coffin from the church after the service.

Flowers and wreaths laid on Elizabeth's grave.

Some of the many mourners examining the wreaths on Elizabeth's grave.

The day after Elizabeth's funeral, memorial services were held at Christ Church, Port Sunlight, at a Mission Meeting in nearby Gladstone Hall, and at St. George's Church in Thornton Hough.

Elizabeth Ellen Lever, Lady Lever, was laid to rest in a simple grave just outside the west end of the church where her effigy and sarcophagus now stand. William apparently always intended this to serve as their final resting place, but the suddenness of her death must have taken everyone by surprise.

The narthex, the elaborate external sandstone canopy which now covers the site of the original grave, was only built after her death.

A sketch of the canopy, known as a narthex, which was later built over the site of Elizabeth's grave.

When Elizabeth laid the foundation stone of Christ Church in September 1902 it had been positioned with the inscription facing inwards, apparently to enable the subsequent construction of the narthex.

The building of this massive superstructure must have been difficult to achieve while still paying due respect to Lady Lever's final resting place.

As well as Elizabeth's remains, its large sand-filled vault now contains those of her husband, the first Lord Leverhulme; of their son William Hulme, the second Lord Leverhulme; and of Lady Freda, William Hulme's second wife.

Over the next two years several memorials were created in Elizabeth's memory.

On May 23rd 1914 the stained glass West Window in Christ Church Port Sunlight, dedicated to her memory, was unveiled by her surviving brother John Hulme. Illustrated on the next page, this large multiple panel window shows 'Christ in the Temple'. On either side are 'The Good Housewife' and 'Ruth and Naomi'. It includes the text *"Whither thou goest I will go"* – a sentiment which in many ways encapsulates the support and encouragement she gave throughout her life to her husband William.

Six months later on December 4th 1914, which would have been Elizabeth's 64th birthday, the narthex and tomb were unveiled by her husband Sir William Lever.

Beneath the canopy of red Shropshire sandstone a marble sarcophagus supports a bronze recumbent effigy of Lady Lever. With two children in bronze at the foot, symbolising her love of children, it was created by the sculptor Sir William Goscombe John.

Lady Lever's head is inclined very slightly to the right, as if waiting for her husband to join her, and on her finger is a ring which local tradition maintains is her original wedding ring. Until the railings were added in later years for security, the ring was always "shiny" where the children had rubbed it for good luck.

Two days after the tomb was unveiled, their son William Hulme Lever unveiled another stained glass window in her memory at St. George's Church in Thornton Hough. It depicts themes similar to the window at Christ Church. The centre panel shows the young Christ in the temple surrounded by the scribes and Pharisees. The left panel shows Naomi being embraced by Ruth while Orpah looks on guiltily. The right panel shows Christ in a house with Mary studying, book in hand at His feet, while Martha brings the food to the table.

In 1936, a third window devoted to her memory, depicting the Resurrection Morning, was donated by their son, William Hulme Lever, to St George's Congregational Church in Bolton where Elizabeth and William were married in April 1874.

On the side of Elizabeth's sarcophagus was a bronze plaque with the epitaph:
"She cultivated only noble thoughts, loving words, and generous deeds".

When William died in 1925 his effigy and sarcophagus were placed right alongside Lady Lever's, obscuring the original plaque which was then removed.

Unveiling of the Lady Lever Memorial Window
Christ Church, Port Sunlight.
May 23rd, 1914

During a dedication service conducted by the Rev L. H. Mills of Christ Church, Port Sunlight, and the Rev T. Langford Burrows of St. George's, Thornton Hough, the memorial window was unveiled by Lady Lever's brother, Mr John Hulme, after which her son, Mr William Hulme Lever, said.........

My father and my uncle have asked me to say a few brief words on their behalf, and on my own, at this service, and I know you will feel for me on this occasion, and know how impossible it is to say at such a time all that one really feels. My father, my uncle, and I know that we are here this evening at the unveiling of a Memorial Window to the best of wives, the truest of sisters, and the fondest of mothers. During all my life, I have never heard my mother give any expression to a single unkind thought, or speak an uncharitable word about anybody. If she knew anything against anybody, she never spoke of it. If she knew anything good about anybody, she never lost a single opportunity of speaking of it to everybody she met. She made it her duty all through her life to bring happiness to everybody who came into contact with her. All that she was to my father, to my uncle, and to me, and to all the members of her family, I assure you no words could possibly explain. In the midst of our sorrow, we must rejoice that, when the end of that beautiful life had to come, my mother was spared the pain of a long illness. It was a serene ending to a life which, I believe, was full of happiness – the happiness which can only come from doing good to others.

St. George's Church,
Thornton Hough

There are three stained-glass windows dedicated to the memory of Lady Elizabeth Ellen Lever:

Illustrated opposite, the largest is the window in Christ Church, Port Sunlight which was unveiled by her brother, John Hulme on May 23rd 1914.

The second window, illustrated above, is in St George's Church, Thornton Hough. It was unveiled by her son, William Hulme Lever, on December 6th 1914.

The third window, from which the detail on the right is taken, was donated by William Hulme Lever to St George's Congregational Church in Bolton where Elizabeth and William were married in April 1874.

St. George's Church,
Bolton

Unveiling of The Narthex and Memorial to Lady Lever, Christ Church, Port Sunlight, December 4th, 1914.

Following a dedication service conducted by the Rev L. H. Mills of Christ Church, and the Rev. T. Langford Burrows of St George's, Thornton Hough, Sir William Lever unveiled the memorial to his wife and said.....

We are endeavouring to-day to give some expression to the great loss we have suffered together in the death of her whose Memorial it is my sorrowing duty to unveil. We wish to perpetuate here in this Village, amidst the people she loved, the memory of Lady Lever. We do not seek to honour her, for it is out of the power of the living to honour the dead. Whatever honour the dead carry with them into their last resting-place, they have won for themselves by their life when on earth, and the living only honour the living in honouring the dead. We can only speak plainly and simply in the language of the heart of her whose resting-place is here. She was loved by all who knew her; and it is more and better to be loved whilst living, than to be honoured after death. And we would be content to leave it so, but we have to consider generations as yet unborn, and who in years to come will live in this village. It is for their sakes, and to fulfil our duty to them that this Memorial has been placed here; for, just as the falling leaf discloses the glorious, ripened fruit and is, in the truest sense, a prophecy of recurring spring-time and harvest, so we would fain reveal to generations to come, her sweet, beautiful, ripened life, and its inspiration, influence and example through succeeding years. All who knew her loved her, for she loved the good and all the good loved her and were made conscious by her gracious sweetness and charm that she had first loved them. No one ever lived who loved others more fully and unselfishly and who loved themselves less. She was ever ready to sacrifice herself to serve others and devoted herself steadfastly to find the good in every one and resolutely refused to think evil of any one. Her warm heart went out in sympathy to all in any sorrow, difficulty or trouble. The suffering turned naturally to her, and the sorrowing sought her loving sympathy; whilst the lonely and desponding placed their hands with confidence in hers and felt encouraged and strengthened as by nothing else. These characteristics had been hers from girlhood's spring-time of life; but as her life matured and ripened they became intensified and there was revealed the richness and depth of her loving nature and the true nobility of her character. We all feel the stronger for her having lived amongst us.

The illustrious artist, the distinguished architect, and the skilled craftsmen have here given of their best with unequalled ability, loving care and devotion. They have here raised their art, profession, and craft to the highest pinnacle of successful accomplishment. In erecting this Memorial to one who ennobled by her life of love and service for others all who knew her, and who has bequeathed the unfading wealth of the memory of her goodness, of her unselfish consecration to duty, her devotion to others, and forgetfulness of self, we are comforted by the thought that death is powerless to rob us of this memory, and that our beloved one requires no finely modelled effigy, nor Gothic masonry, to keep its fragrance for ever sacred in our hearts.

Amidst the changing and decaying scenes of life she beckons us with reassuring loving smile to follow in her footsteps, and tells us we can honour her most by continuing in our lives her deeds of love and service for the living. She rests here amongst those she loved and lived for, and, in due time, I hope I may be privileged to rest beside her.

On this anniversary of the day of her birth, we now with reverence unveil this Memorial to the Glory of God and in praise and gratitude to Him for the beautiful life of Lady Lever, and for the noble example she has bequeathed, to inspire and support us in every call of duty and in every unselfish service of love.

The most striking memorial to Lady Lever must be the Art Gallery which bears her name. Conceived by her husband in 1912 as a display case for his ever growing art collection, it was originally going to be known as 'The Hulme Gallery'.

After the formal laying of the foundation stone by King George V and Queen Mary in March 1914, completion was delayed by the war, and it was finally opened on December 16th 1922 by Princess Beatrice, the youngest daughter of Queen Victoria. In dedicating The Gallery to the memory of his late wife, William said *"Whatever the Gallery may be, it is not sufficient to express the charm of the lady whose memory it will keep green and alive."*

Watched by William, by then Lord Leverhulme, Princess Beatrice performs the ceremony of opening The Gallery.

The fountain known as 'Sea Piece', which stands outside the Gallery, is also a memorial to Lady Lever. Designed by Sir Charles Wheeler, it was commissioned by the Trustees of the Gallery and presented to Lever Brothers to commemorate the one hundredth anniversary of Elizabeth's birth.

'Sea Piece'
This memorial to Elizabeth's birth depicts a legendary seahorse with a triton and baby triton on its back. Water emerges from the tritons' mouths and from two dolphins at the foot of the fountain.

It was unveiled on 5th August 1950 by Elizabeth's grandson Philip, the third Viscount Leverhulme. Born two years after she died, he never knew his grandmother. The idea of the memorial had been conceived by his father who sadly never lived to see it finished.

Portraits of Elizabeth

Although there are many photographs of Elizabeth Ellen Lever, there are only two formally painted portraits of her.

The first, for which sittings took place in London during July 1896, is one of a pair of Elizabeth and William painted by the Liverpool-born artist Sir Luke Fildes. Both of these are now hanging in the Lady Lever Art Gallery at Port Sunlight after being presented to the Gallery by the 3rd Viscount Leverhulme in 1980

William, Elizabeth, and Luke Fildes in Port Sunlight on June 21st 1902

Elizabeth Ellen Lever by Luke Fildes

William Hesketh Lever by Luke Fildes

Seen here on the right, the second portrait of Elizabeth was painted posthumously in 1914 by Maud Hall Neale who was the wife of the artist George Hall Neale. Between them, this husband and wife team painted several portraits of the Lever family.

The painting appears to be based on these two photographs of Elizabeth: Her head and shoulders from a portrait taken in 1912, and the gown and headdress from a picture taken in the Music Room at their Hampstead home, The Hill, in May 1913 by the renowned London photographer, Monsieur Lafayette, albeit a mirror image of the original.

A second portrait sitting three weeks later with Wirral photographer, George Davies, was the basis for this medallion created in readiness for their 40th Wedding anniversary which they would have celebrated the following year.

The medallion includes the initials WHEEL on the reverse - William Hesketh and Elizabeth Ellen Lever.

© Lady Lever Art Gallery

Maude Hall Neale's portrait of Elizabeth

In the background of the portrait are the original pergola, terrace and pond at The Hill.

Elizabeth and a bearded William in 1893

William was a very active Freemason. Seen here in 1908 with William in his masonic regalia, Elizabeth is wearing a silver purse given to her by the officers and members of the William Hesketh Lever Lodge which met in Port Sunlight.
Named after William, the lodge presented Elizabeth with the purse in appreciation of her hosting one of their meetings at Thornton Manor in October 1908.

Elizabeth in 1904 wearing one of the flamboyant gowns which, along with very large hats, she seemed to favour.

Elizabeth with two visitors in the grounds of Thornton Manor

The silver purse was sold to a private buyer in the sale of the contents of Thornton Manor in 2001.

Apart from the two recumbent bronze effigies created by Sir William Gascombe John on the tombs at Christ Church, there are no full-length statues of William or Elizabeth Lever anywhere. There are, however, several head and shoulder 'portrait busts' of them.

The marble busts on the left of William and Elizabeth are by the English sculptor, Edward Onslow Ford. Signed and dated 1900, they are on display in the Lady Lever Art Gallery and stand either side of the entrance to the Leverhulme Room. A plaster copy of Lady Lever's was sold in the Thornton Manor contents sale in 2001.

A posthumous marble bust of Lady Lever was created in 1916 by Sir William Goscombe John. It was sold, together with one of William, in the sale of the Thornton Manor contents in 2001. This marble replica of Lady Lever's is also on display in The Gallery.

© Lady Lever Art Gallery

Mementos of Elizabeth

Elizabeth's writing desk which was sold in the Thornton Manor contents sale in 2001.

Elizabeth's photograph album contains many pictures of her family, but unfortunately none of them have been named.

Elizabeth was a prolific letter writer. This well-used blotter is embossed with her initials, EEL, in silver.

These leather-bound items: a prayer book, hymn book, and carrying case, were a birthday present to Elizabeth from the children of Port Sunlight in December 1908.

When she died Lady Lever was relatively wealthy in her own right. Probate of her personal estate, valued at £18,459 5s 6d, was granted to her husband William, her brother John Hulme, and her son William. Much of her personal wealth was tied up in company shares and her will is very straightforward – everything was left in trust for the benefit of her husband during his lifetime, and thereafter to her son and grandchildren. There are no bequests whatsoever to any other relatives, friends, servants, or charities. Presumably it was assumed that William would take care of all that sort of thing.

Her will was witnessed by George Harley, their Liverpool solicitor, and Sarah Green, described as her housekeeper at Thornton Manor.

During her lifetime, Elizabeth would have had many servants looking after her at all the various houses, but there were only two who were with her for any significant length of time and of whom there are any records: Cecilia Dulston, and Sarah Green, better know to the family as 'Clara'.

At the time of the 1911 census, including Cecilia and Clara, there were fourteen female servants living at Thornton Manor.

Two maids, who were working at Thornton Manor about the time of Elizabeth's death

There are very few photographs of the staff who looked after Elizabeth and William at their various houses. This group, taken at Thornton Manor, includes five gardeners, the estate agent, and six of the female household staff.

Born around 1870 in Liverpool, Cecilia Esther Dulston was a maid. Her whole family were in service. Her Shropshire-born father was a gardener and her brother was a groom and coachman at one of the other large houses in the area. Cecilia first came to work in Thornton Hough as a nurse for the Johnson-Houghton family who lived at nearby Westwood Grange. By 1901 she was the head housemaid in the Lever household at Thornton Manor, a job she held until after Lady Lever's death. One of her regular duties was to wash Elizabeth's hair once a month.

Cecilia also accompanied Elizabeth on several of her foreign trips, presumably acting as her 'lady's maid'. In 1904 she went with her to America, and in 1912 she went with her first to South Africa, and later accompanied her on that long trek through the Congo.

There are no known pictures of Cecilia who never married. After Lady Lever died she continued to live in one of the estate houses looking after her elderly mother, and later moved to live with her brother in America.

Miss Green - 'Clara'

'Clara'

Miss Sarah Green, or as she apparently liked to be known, 'Clara', originally came to work for the Lever family as their housekeeper. She became governess to young William, 'companion' to Elizabeth, and finally housekeeper to William himself.

Clara and Elizabeth were the same age. Outside of the family, she was the one person who featured extensively in Elizabeth's life.

Sarah was born in London on March 11th 1850. Her father, Samuel, was a gunsmith who worked at the Royal Small Arms Factory in Enfield. Why, or when, she adopted the name Clara is not known. Before coming to work for the Lever family she worked as a governess for several other families. In 1871 she was looking after the children of a veterinary surgeon in Banbury, and by 1881, aged 28, she was with the family of a perfumier in her home town of Enfield.

Aged 40, she arrived at Thornton Manor on November 24th 1890 as their housekeeper, although she quickly appears to have combined the role with that of governess for 2-year old William Hulme.

In her diary she described herself as *'Fat and Forty'*. She certainly does not look like that in the early pictures of her with young William who affectionately nicknamed her *'Orders'*, presumably because he thought she bossed him about. She referred to him as *'The little Sunlight Branch'* and *'our little mischievous Sunbeam'*.

Writing of Elizabeth and William, Clara described them *"she in her quiet grace and suavity of manner and he in his true manly nobility, with their natural and mutual devotion to each other and Willie the darling of their hearts, emblematic of the Sunlight of which the inventor is so justly proud."*

They described her as their 'loyal housekeeper, companion, and nanny', and always referred to her as 'Miss Green'.

Elizabeth and Clara being driven through Port Sunlight village.

Clara holding on very tightly to William Hulme at the opening of Victoria Bridge in Port Sunlight in 1897.

Clara and Elizabeth under their parasols at the Sunday School picnic in the gardens of Thornton Manor in 1910.

It has often been suggested that Elizabeth's unnamed companion in this picture is Clara. It is almost certainly not, and is more likely to be a member of the family - possibly William's sister, Alice.

Clara accompanied the family on their first round-the-world trip, lasting from September 1892 to March 1893. They were worried about 4-year old William's health on such a long trip but in her diary Clara wrote that he was *"day by day becoming stronger and more robust, in truth a regular boy promising to have like his father a will of iron combined with his dear mother's quick and forgiving temperament."*

Of William she wrote *"Mr Lever looks much younger than at the commencement of the tour and has lost all sign of his excessive hard work."*

While spending Christmas on the other side of the world in New Zealand she wrote of Elizabeth *"I am rather fond of listening to her words of what we shall do where we shall go when the homecoming time arrives. No mistress of an establishment could love her home with greater truth and sincerity."*

In 1895 Clara went with them again to Australia.

Elizabeth's personal companion for over 20 years, Clara also accompanied her on trips around the United Kingdom, particularly while William was away on business.

Described as *'the esteemed housekeeper and affectionate friend of all at Thornton Manor'*, after Elizabeth died in 1913 Clara continued as housekeeper at The Manor.

In May 1919 'Miss Green' moved with William, who was by then Lord Leverhulme, to be his housekeeper at The Hill, where she passed away just five months later in October, aged 69.

She was laid to rest in the nearby Hampstead Cemetery where her gravestone is simply inscribed -

In
Loving Memory
of
Sarah Green, "Clara".
Born March 11ᵗʰ 1850,
Died October 27ᵗʰ 1919.

Clara's grave in Hampstead Cemetery.

Clara with Elizabeth on the terrace in front of The Bungalow at Rivington

On July 6th 1911, two years before Elizabeth died, William was made a Baronet in the coronation honours list for King George V. He became Sir William Hesketh Lever, and Elizabeth became Lady Lever. This picture shows the proud couple soon after the award was made.

This Pigeon Tower is now the only building left intact on The Bungalow site at Rivington. Elizabeth is said to have used the upper room for sewing and practicing her musical instruments. It stands high above the Lancashire plain - a memorial to those who once lived here.

"I venture to say that without the gracious influence of my wife I doubt whether there would have been a Port Sunlight….. nor a Lever Brothers as we know it today. It came because of the confidence she inspired in me."

Lord Leverhulme speaking at the opening of the Lady Lever Gallery. December 17th 1922

Seen here aged just 35, Elizabeth Ellen Lever, Lady Lever, was in her sixty-third year when she died, relatively young by modern standards. Beset by family tragedies in her younger life, she had married the man she loved who went on to become perhaps the greatest industrialist of his time. From relatively simply beginnings in Bolton, at a time when ladies often did not go far from their home town, she and William travelled the world together. She lived from the time of horse drawn cabs to motor cars. She never travelled by aeroplane, and took her first ride on a Tube train in 1908.

She often questioned her own worthiness, but believed deeply in the will of God, and rarely missed attending church on a Sunday. She loved children and sadly only lived to see one of her grandchildren, Elizabeth Ruth, born in April 1913, recording excitedly *"Now I am a Grannie"*. She learnt to ride, enjoyed knitting and even made attempts to play musical instruments, all with apparently varying success.

She was a prolific letter writer and in later life she was obliged to wear glasses – perhaps as a result of the amount of writing she did. She was a keen home-maker and enjoyed the company of her own family, but above all she supported her husband in all he undertook, was immensely proud of her son, and was sorely missed by everyone when she passed away.

Further Reading

- ***Viscount Leverhulme by His Son.***
  William's biography, written by their son, William Hulme Lever, and published two years after his father's death.   George Allen & Unwin Ltd. London. 1927

- ***Following The Flag - Jottings of a Jaunt Round the World.***
  A record of Elizabeth and William's first voyage around the world between September 1892 and March 1893, which originally appeared in the form of letters to the Birkenhead News.   Simpkin Marshall & Co. Ltd. 1893

- ***Men of Stress.***
  An in-depth examination of William's life and business alongside those of the self-made American steel tycoon and philanthropist Andrew Carnegie and President Woodrow Wilson.   Harley Williams. Alden Press Oxford. 1948

- ***Edwardian Portraits.***
  An account of the Edwardian Age by William Scovell Adams which includes a biography of William together with Baden-Powell, and Edward VII.
  W.S.Adams. Secker & Warburg, London. 1957

- ***Lord Leverhulme: A Biography.*** One of several very readable biographies of emminent men written by Professor Jolley.   W.P.Jolley. Constable, London. 1976

- ***Coming Clean.***
  An autobiography of Andrew Knox who, from a junior position in Lever Brothers, became a board member and was personally acquainted with William.
  A.M.Knox. Heinemann. 1976

- ***Art and Business in Edwardian England. The Making of The Lady Lever Art Gallery.***
  Edward Morris. (ed.) National Museums and Galleries on Merseyside. 1992

- ***Leverhulme's Rivington .***
  A comprehensive illustrated history of The Bungalow and Rivington Estate.
  M.D.Smith. Wyre Publishing. 1998

- ***My Aunt Edith.***
  A biography of the suffragette, Edith Rigby, who set fire to The Bungalow.
  Phoebe Hesketh. Plymouth. 1966

- ***A Pictorial History of Port Sunlight. 1988 – 1953.***
  Gavin Hunter & Ian Boumphrey. 2002

- ***The King of Sunlight.***
  'How William Lever Cleaned Up The World.' Another well written biography of William with some interesting commentaries on his various activities.
  Adam Macqueen. Transworld Publishers. 2004

- ***So Clean.***
  A slightly unorthodox biography of William placing him within the social, cultural and economic context of his time.   Brian Lewis. Manchester University Press. 2008

1820 Oct 20th	Elizabeth's father, Crompton Hulme, was born in Little Lever.
1827 Apr 9th	Elizabeth's mother, Margaret Pearson, was born in Darcy Lever.
1839 Apr 10th	William's father, James Lever, married Eliza Hesketh, in Manchester.
1840 Mar 31st	William's sister, Elizabeth Lever, was born in Manchester.
1841	Crompton Hulme was still an apprentice draper under Mr Thomas Scholes.
1841 Nov 9th	William's sister, Eliza Emma Lever, was born in Manchester.
1842	The Lever family moved from Manchester to Wood Street, Bolton.
1842 July 25th	Crompton Hulme's sister Betty married Margaret's brother John.
1843 Aug 14th	William's sister, Mary Lever, was born in Wood Street.
1845 May 20th	Crompton's father, John Hulme, died aged 67.
1845 Sept 30th	William's sister, Jane Lever, was born in Wood Street.
1845 Dec 9th	Elizabeth's maternal grandmother, Ellen Pearson, died aged 47.
1847 Oct 11th	William's sister, Emily Lever, was born in Wood Street.
1847 Dec 11th	Crompton's sister, Ann Cranshaw, died aged 39.
1848 Jan 27th	Elizabeth's parents, Margaret Pearson and Crompton Hulme, were married.
1849 June 21st	William's youngest sister, Elizabeth Lever, died aged 9 years.
1849 Aug 31st	William's sister, Alice Lever, was born in Wood Street.
1850	Crompton and Margaret Hulme were living in Deansgate, Bolton.
1850 Dec 4th	**Elizabeth Ellen Hulme was born in Deansgate, Bolton.**
1851 Sept 19th	**William Hesketh Lever was born in Wood Street, Bolton.**
1852 Oct 31st	Elizabeth's sister, Betsy Hulme, was born in Deansgate.
1854 Jan 13th	Elizabeth's sister, Betsy Hulme, died aged 14 months.
1854 Feb 10th	William's only brother, James Darcy Lever, was born in Wood Street, Bolton.
1855 May 21st	Elizabeth's brother, John Hulme, was born in Deansgate.
1855 Dec 1st	William's younger sister, Hariette Lever, was born in Wood Street.
1856 Nov 3rd	Crompton's brother, George Hulme, died aged 41.
1857 Jan 30th	Crompton's married sister, Mary Allen, died aged 54.
1857	William, aged 6, started at the Misses Aspinwall's School in Wood Street.
1857 Sept 2nd	Elizabeth's sister, Mary Jane Hulme, was born.
1857 Dec 6th	Elizabeth's sister, Mary Jane Hulme, died aged 3 months at Deansgate.
1858 Feb 25th	William's youngest sister, Lucy Ann Lever, was born in Wood Street.
1859 Aug 1st	Elizabeth's brother George Hulme, was born in Deansgate.
1860	The Hulme family had moved to No.15 Wood Street.
1860	Crompton's sister, Sarah, who had already been widowed, re-married.
1860 June 17th	Elizabeth's brother, George Hulme, died aged 10 months, at Wood Street.
1860	William Lever moved from the Misses Aspinwall's School to Kay's School.
1862 Sept 25th	Elizabeth's brother, James Crompton Hulme, was born.
1863 Aug 24th	Elizabeth's father, Crompton Hulme, died aged 42 at Wood Street.
1864	William Lever moved from Kay's School to the Church Institute.
1864 June	The Lever family moved away to live above the wholesale warehouse.
1866 Feb 24th	Crompton Hulme's mother, Elizabeth's grandmother, Betty died aged 86.
1866	Elizabeth had moved to Southport with her mother and two brothers.
1867 June 29th	William began his apprenticeship in his father's business.
1872	William was made a partner in the family grocery business.

Chronology

1872 Dec 7th	**Elizabeth and William announced their engagement.**
1873 May 8th	The Lever family moved to a new home at Harwood Lodge.
1873 June	Elizabeth, her mother, and her two brothers moved back to Bolton.
1873 July 2nd	Elizabeth's mother, Margaret Hulme, died in Bolton aged 46.
1874 April 15th	**Elizabeth Ellen Hulme married William Hesketh Lever.**
1875 Feb 3rd	Elizabeth gave birth to a still-born daughter at Park Street.
1876 Oct 1st	Elizabeth gave birth to a still-born son at Park Street.
1877 Aug 24th	Elizabeth gave birth to their second still-born son at Park Street.
1877	William established the Wigan Branch of Lever & Co.
1878 Jan	Elizabeth and William went on a trip to France for two weeks.
1879	Elizabeth and William moved to Lower House on Chorley New Road in Bolton.
1882 Dec 21st	Elizabeth's baby daughter, Elizabeth, died just 3 hours old in Wigan.
1884	Elizabeth and William went on a Summer cruise together around the Scottish islands.
1885 Apr 22nd	Elizabeth's brother John Hulme married Alice Holt.
1885 Aug	William and his brother James founded Lever Brothers.
1885 Aug 14th	Elizabeth gave birth to their third daughter, Elizabeth Hulme Lever.
1885 Aug 23rd	Baby Elizabeth Hulme was buried in Heaton Cemetery, Bolton aged 4 days.
1886 Jan 20th	Crompton Hulme's married sister, Sarah Allen, died aged 74.
1886 Oct 31st	Elizabeth attended the dedication of the extension to Stand Chapel.
1887 Aug	Elizabeth and William went with friends on a caravan tour of the West Country.
1888 Mar 3rd	Elizabeth cut the first sod marking the start of Port Sunlight factory.
1888 Mar 25th	Elizabeth and William's son William Hulme Lever was born at 'Westcombe', Bolton.
1888 Apr 30th	William Hulme Lever was baptised at 'Westcombe'.
1888 Sept	Elizabeth and William moved into Thornton Manor as tenants of the Forwood family.
1889 Mar 15th	Elizabeth's brother's wife, Alice Hulme died aged 34.
1890 Nov 24th	Clara Green arrived at Thornton Manor as 'Housekeeper'.
1890 Aug 23rd	Elizabeth and William went with employees to Beaumaris to celebrate the completion of the first phase of the Port Sunlight factory.
1891 Apr 15th	Elizabeth's still-born baby was buried at Heaton cemetery, Bolton.
1891 Dec 1st	Elizabeth and William set off for a six-week holiday in Egypt.
1892 Sept 14th	Elizabeth and William set off aboard SS Germanic for a round-the-world trip.
1893 Mar 9th	Elizabeth and William returned from their world trip.
1893 Apr 18th	William bought Thornton Manor.
1893 Nov 28th	William's mother, Eliza Lever, died at Harwood aged 75.
1893 Dec 12th	Elizabeth and William began using their Hyde Park Court apartment.
1894 May	William's spinster sisters, Emily, Alice, and Harriette, together with their widowed father, moved from Harwood to Thornton Hough.
1894 Sept	Elizabeth and William began using their new home in Norfolk Street, London.
1895 Mar 13th	Elizabeth and William left from Liverpool for a six-week trip to America.
1895 Sept	William's widowed sister, Eliza Bromiley, moved to Thornton Hough
1895 Sept 21st	Elizabeth, William, and their son left Southampton for a trip to Australia.
1895 Dec 27th	Elizabeth cut the first sod of the Balmain oil mill in Australia.
1896 Feb 7th	Elizabeth and William returned early from the trip because of the illness of William's brother, James.
1896 July	Elizabeth had eleven sittings for the portrait painted by Luke Fildes.

1896 Oct 8th	Elizabeth and William set out on a six-week visit to America and Canada.
1897 Apr14th	Elizabeth and William moved back into Thornton Manor after extensive alterations .
1897 Aug 1st	Elizabeth and William set out on a three week visit to Switzerland.
1897 Sept 19th	Elizabeth and William spent their last night at their Norfolk Street home.
1897 May 26th	William's father, James Lever, died in Thornton Hough aged 87.
1898 Jan 9th	Elizabeth and William went on a two week visit to Switzerland
1898 Feb 18th	William's brother, James Darcy Lever, retired due to ill health.
1898 Feb 21st	William purchased 'Hillside, their new home in Bolton.
1899 Feb13th	They spent their first night at 'Hillside'.
1899 Mar 8th	Elizabeth and William set out for a visit to America and Canada.
1899 Apr 27th	Elizabeth and William arrived back at Hillside from their transatlantic trip.
1899 Oct 18th	Elizabeth and William moved back into Thornton Manor after more alterations.
1900 Mar 23rd	William's bid to buy the Rivington Estate near Bolton was accepted.
1900 Sept 8th	Elizabeth laid the foundation stone of Deane Congregational Mission, Bolton.
1900 Oct 12th	Elizabeth went with William on a six-day visit to Paris.
1900 Dec 5th	Elizabeth opened Chorley Old Road Congregational Church, Bolton.
1901 Jul 31st	Elizabeth and William went together for a fortnight to The Crown Hotel, Harrogate.
1901 Sept 12th	Elizabeth and William set out together for another round-the-world trip.
1901 Dec 18th	Elizabeth and William returned 94 days later from their world trip.
1902 Jan 23rd	Elizabeth and William began using Roynton Cottage, "The Bungalow", at Rivington.
1902 Feb 19th	Elizabeth opened The Blackburn Road Sunday School, Bolton.
1902 June 27th	Elizabeth opened an extension to Pennant House Grounds near Port Sunlight.
1902 Sept 30th	Elizabeth laid the foundation stone of Christ Church, Port Sunlight.
1903 Apr 10th	Elizabeth laid the foundation stone of Edgeworth Congregational School, Bolton.
1904 Jan 27th	Elizabeth set out with William on a six-week visit to America.
1904 Apr 29th	Elizabeth's brother, James Hulme, died aged 41.
1904 June 8th	Elizabeth formally opened Christ Church, Port Sunlight.
1904 July 28th	Elizabeth accompanied William on a four-week visit to America.
1904 Sept 22nd	Elizabeth left with William for a two-week trip to Germany.
1905 July 24th	Elizabeth and William finally moved into their new home at The Hill', Hampstead.
1906 Jan 24th	William was elected Liberal MP for Wirral.
1906 Feb 17th	Elizabeth opened the Hoylake and West Kirby Cottage Hospital on Wirral.
1906 Apr 11th	Elizabeth laid the foundation stone of St George's Church, Thornton Hough.
1906 May 18th	Elizabeth opened the New Congregational Church at Hoylake, Wirral.
1906 June 15th	Elizabeth opened Moreton Presbyterian Church on Wirral.
1906 Sept 20th	Elizabeth laid the foundation stone of the new schools at the Primitive Methodist Church in Seacombe, Wirral.
1907 May 29th	Elizabeth opened St George's Church, Thornton Hough.
1908 June12th	Elizabeth laid the foundation stone of the Congregational Church, Birkenhead.
1908 June 27th	Elizabeth laid a foundation stone at Neston Wesleyan Church and Schools.
1910 Mar 16th	Elizabeth went with William on a twelve-day trip to Holland and France.
1910 Mar 29th	William's brother James Darcy Lever died at Thornton Hough.
1910 Aug 25th	Elizabeth launched SS Kulambanga at old Kilpatrick, Glasgow.
1911 July 6th	Elizabeth became Lady Lever when William was made a Baronet.

Chronology

1912 Jan 6th	Elizabeth and William left Southampton for a visit to South Africa.
1912 Feb 7th	Elizabeth cermonially cut the first sod of the Capetown works.
1912 Feb 24th	Elizabeth and William returned from their South African trip.
1912 Apr 24th	Elizabeth and William attended their son William Hulme's wedding in Chorley.
1912 Apr 25th	Elizabeth and William left for a ten-day visit to France & Germany.
1912 Nov 16th	Elizabeth and William sailed from Antwerp aboard the SS Leopoldville for Africa.
1913 Mar 10th	Elizabeth and William returned to Thornton Manor from their trip to the Congo.
1913 Apr 9th	Elizabeth and William's first grandchild, Elizabeth Ruth Lever, was born.
1913 Apr 29th	Elizabeth was elected a Fellow of the Royal Geographical Society.
1913 May 10th	Elizabeth left with William for a week's visit to Paris and Brussels.
1913 June 28th	Elizabeth and William hosted a garden party at Thornton Manor.
1913 July 7th	Elizabeth and William dined with the King and Queen at Lord Derby's home.
1913 July 8th	The Bungalow at Rivington was destroyed in an arson attack.
1913 July 10th	Elizabeth and William attended the visit by the King and Queen to Bolton.
1913 July 19th	Elizabeth and William attended a garden party at their son's home.
1913 July 24th	**Elizabeth Ellen, Lady Lever died at Thornton Manor**
1913 July 26th	Lady Lever's funeral took place at Christ Church, Port Sunlight
1914 Mar 24th	The foundation stone of The Lady Lever Gallery, Port Sunlight, was laid by King George VI and Queen Mary.
1914 May 23rd	The stained glass west window in Christ Church, Port Sunlight, dedicated to Elizabeth's memory, was unveiled by her brother, John Hulme.
1914	Maud Hall Neile painted a posthumous portrait of Elizabeth.
1914 Dec 4th	Elizabeth's tomb at Christ Church Port Sunlight was unveiled by her husband Sir William Lever.
1914 Dec 6th	The stained glass window in Elizabeth's memory at St George's Church in Thornton Hough was unveiled by their son William Hulme Lever.
1917 June 21st	William became Baron Leverhulme of Bolton-le-Moors.
1919 Oct 27th	Elizabeth's friend and companion Clara Green died at The Hill, London.
1922 Nov 27th	William became Viscount Leverhulme of the Western Isles.
1922 Dec 16th	The Lady Lever Gallery in Port Sunlight was opened by Princess Beatrice, youngest daughter of Queen Victoria.
1925 May 7th	**William Hesketh Lever, Viscount Leverhulme, died at The Hill, London.**
1935 Jan 25th	Elizabeth's last surviving brother, John Hulme, died aged 80.
1949 May 27th	William Hulme Lever, the 2nd Lord Leverhulme died.
1950 Aug 5th	The Memorial Fountain, 'Sea Spirit', in Port Sunlight was unveiled by Elizabeth's grandson, Philip William Bryce Lever, the 3rd Viscount Leverhulme.
2000 July 4th	Philip William Bryce Lever, the 3rd Viscount Leverhulme died.